WINDOWS 95 LIFERAFT

The publisher offers discounts on this book when ordered in quantity. For more information please contact:

Special Sales Department
Manning Publications Co.
3 Lewis Street
Greenwich, CT 06830
or
lee@manning.com
Fax: (203) 661–9018

Copyediting: Margaret Marynowski
Typesetting: Dorothy Marsico
Internal Design: Frank Cunningham
Cover Design: Fernando Gonzalez Bunster

Library of Congress Cataloging in Publication Data

Richardson, Ronny.
Windows 95 liferaft / Ronny Richardson.
p. cm.
Includes index.
ISBN 1-884777-20-1
1. Microsoft Windows (Computer file) 2. Operating systems (Computers) I. Title.
QA76.76.O63R5438 1996
005.4'469--dc20 96-15536
CIP

1 2 3 4 5 6 7 8 9 10—CR—00 99 98 97 96

Windows 95 Liferaft

RONNY RICHARDSON

MANNING
Greenwich
(74° w. long.)

Acknowledgments

Personally, I want to thank my wife Cicinda, my son Tevin, and my daughter Dawna for their support and patience. Because I have only a limited pool of time available, some of the time I spent writing this book had to come from the time I would have spent with my family. They were all very understanding and supportive.

Professionally, I want to thank Marjan Bace at Manning Publications. This book was his idea. He not only came up with the book idea, he pushed hard to get it published quickly so I would have the time to write without having to rush. Without him, you would not be reading this book today.

Contents

Introduction

If Windows 95 is so easy to use, why are the books on Windows 95 so big? If Windows 95 is so easy to use, why do so many of the books on Windows 95 make you feel like such a dummy for buying them?

This book is not like other Windows 95 books. I am not going to tell you how to do any of the following:

- Install Windows 95.
- Tweak Windows 95 to get it to perform some little known trick of questionable value.
- Make Windows 95 do something it was never designed to do in the first place.

If you are looking for a book on any of these topics, you should immediately put this book down and grab another one. Look for one of the "fat" ones. The heavier the better. Not only is there a good chance it will have just the trick you want, you will also get in shape just by lifting it.

Now that everyone looking for a monster Windows 95 book has left, I will tell you about this book. But first, let me tell you a secret. Windows 95 is really very easy to use! No, really, it is! This book contains everything you need to know to use Windows 95 effectively and productively.

About this Book

Most computer books are written by computer jocks who have learned to use dozens or even hundreds of other software packages and who don't have a clue how the rest of us learn to use software. They got a copy of Windows 95 while it was still being tested (this is called *beta testing*), and they rushed to learn to use it with little or no documentation. In the little time they had remaining before their deadlines, they frantically tried to throw everything they learned into their book. With all this frantic rushing, they barely had time to get the books written. As a result, they could not take the time to think about the typical reader and decide what he really needs to know.

This book is different. I am a schoolteacher, not a computer jock. I routinely teach introductory computer courses to students who have never used a computer. As a result, I have a lot of experience teaching people how to use computers. I know what to gloss over and what to spend a lot of time explaining. I also know how to explain it without making you feel like a dummy and without burying you under a mountain of computer terms.

In addition, I have taken my time in writing this book. Many of the other Windows 95 books on the shelf were there well before this one. However, computer books are like fine wine. The first ones finished are rarely the best ones. I think you will find that the extra time and care that

I have taken in crafting this book will make it a much more useful book to you.

How to use this Book

This book begins at the very beginning and moves forwards. If you already have some experience with computers and any version of Windows, you may want to skip the first chapter. Keep in mind, this is not a novel. You can skip the sections you are familiar with and skim sections you think you know. If you find out later that you missed something, you can always refer back to the appropriate section.

How this Book is Structured

What follows is a brief discussion of the chapters of this book:

Chapter 1: In The Beginning....
This chapter describes what goes on when you first turn on the computer—a process called *booting*. It also explains the "right" way to turn off Windows 95.

Chapter 2: The Windows 95 Interface
This is perhaps the most important chapter in the book. It explains the overall approach Windows 95 takes to its operation. You will learn about menus, windows, dialog boxes, and much more.

Chapter 3: Working With Programs
This chapter shows you how to start one or more programs and how to switch between multiple programs. After all, you have Windows 95 to run programs, not to run Windows 95. It also gives a brief tour of the programs that come with Windows 95.

Chapter 4: The Windows 95 Productivity Programs
This chapter shows you how to use the Windows 95 programs that can help you get your work done.

Chapter 5: The Windows 95 Recreational Programs
This chapter shows you how to use the Windows 95 programs that can help you have fun.

Chapter 6: Organizing And Managing Your Files
This chapter shows you how to manage the files on your computer using built-in Windows 95 tools.

Chapter 7: Sharing Information
This chapter shows you how to use Windows 95 to share information between programs.

Chapter 8: Getting Help
This chapter shows you how to use the help system to find out how to use any program.

Last Notes

I certainly hope it does not happen. I've done everything I know of to keep it from happening. However, it is possible that you will get lost at some point while reading this book or you will fail to understand something. If this happens, please make a note and drop me a line. Tell me what you did not understand and why. If you are too confused to clearly state the problem, then let me know where I started to lose you.

I have a very selfish reason for asking you to do this. I want to keep this book in print as long as there is a market for it. If you help me spot the confusing portions, I can work on them and make the next edition even better. In addition, knowing where I failed to clearly explain something will help me as I write other books. I'll add the usual disclaimer that I can't always respond to individual letters in case I get a surge of letters; however, I have managed so far. The address is:

RONNY RICHARDSON

c/o Manning Publications Company
3 Lewis Street
Greenwich, Connecticut 06830

If you are active in the on-line community, you can reach me on CompuServe, where my address is:

70322,3100 or
70322.3100@compuserve.com

You can also visit my home page at:

http://www.quincy.edu/~richaro/

The best way to reach me is on-line.

CHAPTER 1

In the Beginning...

When you turn on a computer, it begins something called *booting*. Booting is the process of getting the computer ready for you to use. During most of this process, you will see the blue sky with white clouds background of Windows 95 on the screen. The following is what the computer and then Windows 95 goes through while booting:

1. *The computer checks the memory, the hard disk, and other components.* While the computer is checking the memory, you may see a counter on the screen.
2. *The computer loads some simple Windows 95 files from the hard disk.* These files simply continue the booting process.
3. *Windows 95 scans the computer for Plug and Play components.* These are special hardware components for newer computers that automatically configure themselves.
4. *If everything is okay to this point—and it usually is—the computer loads the rest of Windows 95.*

5. *If you have a CONFIG.SYS file or an AUTOEXEC.BAT file, Windows 95 processes these.*
6. *If your computer is connected to a network, then Windows 95 loads the appropriate drivers.* You may need to enter a password at this point.
7. *Windows 95 loads any programs you have specified in your StartUp group.* These are programs you have told Windows 95 to run automatically each time it starts.

➤The CONFIG.SYS and AUTOEXEC .BAT configuration files are from the pre-Windows 95 days. If you don't have them, you don't need them.

At this point, Windows 95 has finished booting and is waiting for you to tell it what to do. Depending on how fast of a computer you have, how many items are in your CONFIG.SYS and AUTOEXEC.BAT files, and how many programs you have in your StartUp group, this could take several minutes.

The Windows 95 Screen

➤If you do not see the Taskbar at the bottom of the screen, move the mouse cursor to the bottom and see if it appears. You can configure the Taskbar to stay hidden until the mouse cursor is near it.

Windows 95 presents the user with an easy to use interface. Figure 1-1 shows Windows 95 as it might look when it first starts. Since Windows 95 can be configured in many different ways, the version you have might look different from this. We will begin by exploring the parts of this screen.

➤To change the name of your computer, right-click on the "My Computer" icon and select Rename from the menu that pops up. Pick a name that is special to you.

Ronny's Computer: Unless you have changed its name as I have, this icon will say "My Computer" on your system. This lists the files, programs, folders, and hardware you have. Double click on this icon and it will open a window similar to Fig-

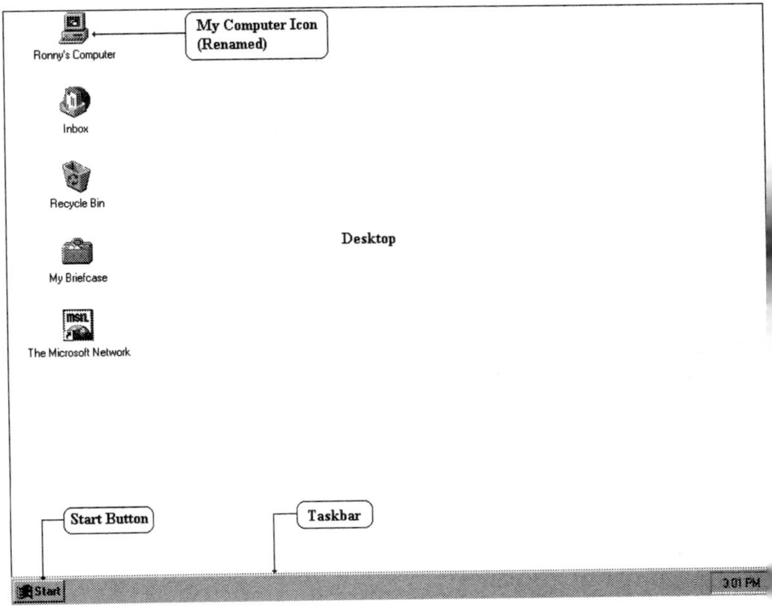

Figure 1–1: **A typical Windows 95 opening screen.**

ure 1–2 showing all the drives you have (A–G on my computer) as well as other information we will discuss later.

Network Neighborhood: You do not see this icon in Figure 1–1 since I am not connected to a network. If you are connected to a network, there will be an icon labeled Network Neighborhood that you can double click on to access all the computers and printers to which you are networked.

Inbox: This is where you will find incoming e-mail. Using this requires you to be a member of Microsoft Network or to have

►*Microsoft Fax requires that you have a modem that can double as a fax machine.*

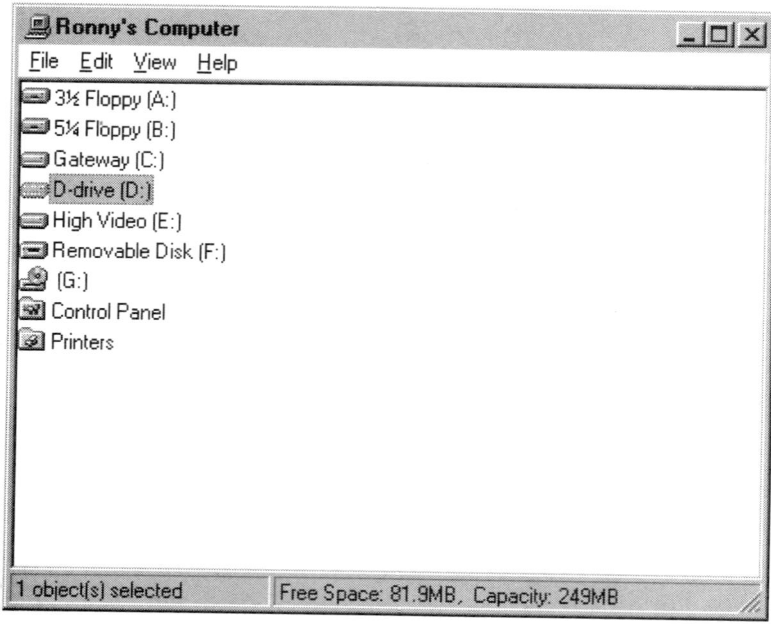

Figure 1–2: **The window you get by double-clicking on the "My Computer" icon.**

► Microsoft Mail requires that you be part of a network.

►Saving old files protects you from losing a file by accidently deleting it since you can always get it back.

a modem to use Microsoft Mail or Microsoft Fax.

Recycle Bin: When you tell Windows 95 to delete a file, Windows 95 appears to remove it from your computer. However, it simply places the file in the Recycle Bin. At anytime in the future, up to when you "empty" the trash or the trash gets full, you can recover the file. Once you open the Recycle Bin and empty the trash, you cannot get your files back. Note that Windows 95 does not use the Recycle Bin if you use an older program to erase a file. It also does not store temporary or working files that programs create and erase in the Recycle Bin.

My Briefcase: This is a Windows 95 tool that lets you group files together to move them between computers. This can be useful if you have a desktop and notebook computer or a computer at the office and another one at home.

►*In order to use the Briefcase, both computers must use Windows 95.*

The Microsoft Network: The Microsoft Network is an on-line service of Microsoft. It offers discussion areas, e-mail, shareware software, and more. Using this service is not free. It requires that you have a modem and pay to use the service.

►*There are competing services, such as CompuServe and America Online, that offer a broader range of services than does Microsoft Network.*

As you can see from Figure 1–1, Windows 95 is very visual in nature. It places a lot of graphical images on the screen. You can perform many tasks in Windows 95 by pointing to and manipulating these graphical images. Since Windows 95 is visual in nature, it is often called a *graphical user interface* or GUI, pronounced "gooey."

A graphical user interface has a significant advantage, especially for new users. Without a GUI, you would have to type in commands for the computer to execute. In addition, you would have to deal with arcane error messages when you entered a command incorrectly or when the computer encountered a problem. However, with a GUI you simply point to pictures on the screen, click or double-click on them, or drag them to a new location. When the computer needs more information, it displays a dialog box and allows you to click on the appropriate button or make a selection from a list.

Controlling Windows 95

➤The Microsoft Plus! Package you can purchase to go with Windows 95 lets you pick from a variety of cursors.

The most common way to communicate with Windows 95 is using a mouse. As you move the mouse across your desktop, a small on-screen pointer tracks it movement. This on-screen pointer is the *mouse pointer* or *cursor*. Move the mouse left, right, forwards, or backwards and the mouse pointer moves in the same direction.

Most mice have two buttons on them, the left and right button. The majority of your actions in Windows 95 use the left mouse button. A few mice have three buttons. You rarely use the center button on these mice.

If you are left-handed, you can tell Windows 95 to switch the buttons so the right button performs the actions of the left button, and vice-versa. The steps to do that are as follows:

1. Click on the start button.
2. Highlight Settings.
3. Click on Control Panel.
4. Double-click on Mouse.
5. Under Button Configuration, click on Left-Handed.

➤ Mouse pads come with a wide variety of designs. Picking a unique mouse pad is a great way to customize your desktop. My mouse pad has a picture of my family.

A mouse typically sits on a *mouse pad* to give it additional traction. If you move the mouse to the edge of the mouse pad and need to continue moving in that direction, you can pick the mouse up and move it back to the center of the pad. While the mouse is in the air and not touching the surface, the mouse pointer will not move as you move the mouse.

You pick items in Windows 95 by moving the mouse pointer until its tip is on the center of the picture of the item you wish to select. This is called *pointing*. The various pictures you see on the screen are *icons*.

You work with icons and other Windows 95 elements in one of four ways: *clicking*, *double-clicking*, *dragging*, and *right-clicking*. To click on an icon, you point to that icon with the mouse pointer and press and release the left mouse button. Clicking selects an icon or window and opens a menu.

➤*For users upgrading from Windows 3.1, right-clicking is one of the more useful features of Windows 95.*

You double-click by pointing to an icon with the mouse cursor and pressing and releasing the left mouse button twice in rapid succession. You must do this very rapidly in order for Windows 95 to see it as a double-click rather than just two clicks.

If you are having trouble double-clicking fast enough, you can instruct Windows 95 to give you more time to double-click. That is, you can tell it to allow more time between two single-clicks where it will count them as a double-click. The steps to do this are as follows:

1. Click on the Start button.
2. Highlight Settings.
3. Click on Control Panel.
4. Double-click on Mouse.
5. Under Double-Click Speed, change the slider to the desired value.

Dragging is typically used to move something. You drag by first pointing to the icon or other Windows 95 element with the mouse cursor. Next, press the left mouse button but do not release it. You can then move the mouse cursor to a new location. You then release the mouse button to finish dragging. You right-click by pointing to an icon or other element and clicking with the right mouse button. This is typically used to display an item-specific menu of actions you can take.

➤ *Many menu items show the equivalent keyboard shortcut right on the menu beside the name of the command. Reading the menus is an excellent way to learn keyboard shortcuts.*

You can accomplish most of the actions you take with the mouse using keystroke combinations on the keyboard. These are called *keyboard shortcuts*. These are typically harder to perform than using the mouse and most users rarely use them so I will not cover them. They are called shortcuts only because they allow you to work without removing your hands from the keyboard.

Quitting Windows 95

We will see how to control Windows 95 in the next chapter. However, it is very important that you know how to stop Windows 95 so we are going to cover that in this first chapter.

Where Did The Start Button Go?

You may find yourself working on a system that appears to lack the Start button you see in Figure 1–1. The reason is simple. The Start button takes up a lot of screen space—even when you are not using it. Windows 95 allows you to avoid this by telling the Start button to disappear when you are not using it. To make it reappear, simply move the mouse cursor to the bottom of the screen and pause for a second or so. Directly, the Start button will appear and you can use it normally. If you move the mouse cursor away from the bottom of the screen, the Start button will assume you are finished with it and disappear again.

Windows 95 performs a lot of tasks in the background. If you simply turn off your computer when you finish, you might interrupt some of these background tasks. In addition, Windows 95 creates temporary work files on your hard disk. Normally, it erases these, but if you turn off the computer without giving it a chance, they end up cluttering up your hard disk and taking up space. To avoid problems, always shut down Windows 95 properly.

►For the same reason, you should be careful to always use the Shut Down option of the Start menu when you want to reboot your computer or restart Windows 95.

To properly shut down Windows 95, perform the following steps:

1. Click on the Start button.
2. Select Shut Down from the Start menu. Windows 95 will give you the option of shutting down or restarting.
3. Select Shutting Down and click on OK.

Windows 95 will perform some housekeeping and then tell you when it is safe to turn off the computer.

Conclusion

You now know your way around the Windows 95 screen. You know what the computer does while it is booting and you know how to exit Windows 95.

CHAPTER 2

The Windows 95 Interface

If you look back at Figure 1–1, you will see that most of the screen is blank. This blank area is the *desktop*. The desktop is the surface you use to work on with the computer, just as your office desktop is the surface you use to work on in your office.

The Start Menu

Most of the time, you start a program in Windows 95 using the Start menu. The Start menu is different from every other Windows 95 menu. You do not display it by clicking on a name at the top of the screen. Rather, you display it by clicking on the Start button at the bottom of the screen. This brings up the menu shown in Figure 2–1. This also shows another difference in the Start menu. It pops up, rather than dropping down.

►If you do not see the Start Button, move the cursor to the bottom of the screen. Many users configure Windows 95 to show the Start Button when you move the cursor to the bottom.

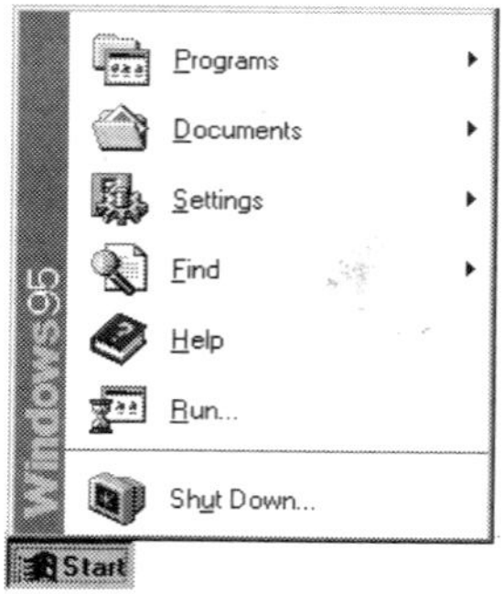

Figure 2–1: **You use the Start button to launch a program.**

If the cascaded menus do not appear when you highlight them, single-click on the menu option.

The Start menu is a cascading menu. As you highlight each menu option, a submenu automatically appears. Figure 2–2 shows a typical submenu. Typically, you use the Start button to start a program. This is called *launching* the program. To start a program, highlight Programs in the Start menu. This will display a cascaded menu like the one shown in Figure 2–3. Of course, your menu will depend on the programs you have purchased.

You can configure the Start menu to require you to click before showing a cascaded menu.

Arrows mean you will get another menu.

The menu in Figure 2–3 consists of two different types of entries. The entries at the top with arrows beside them are cascaded menus where similar programs have been grouped together. For example, the third entry in Figure 2–3 contains all the programs I use for maintenance. These include a backup program and the Norton Utilities. The entries without arrows

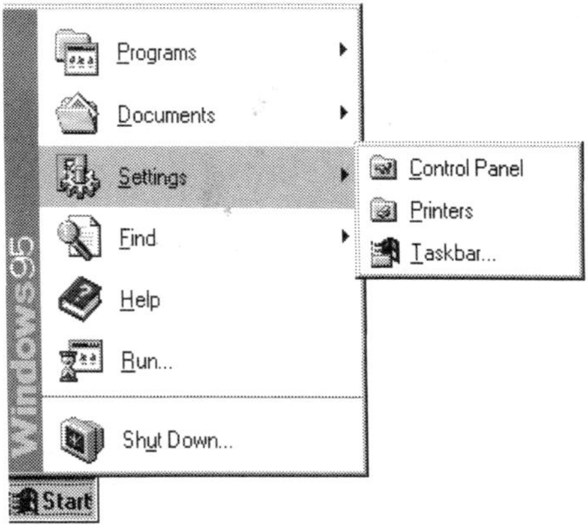

Figure 2–2: **Highlighting a menu item brings up a submenu.**

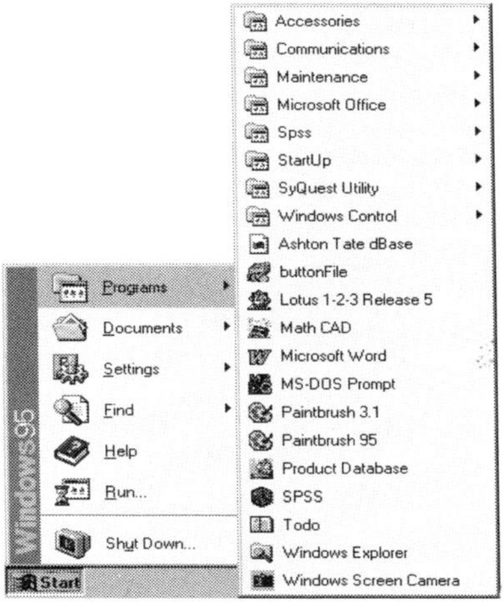

Figure 2–3: **The cascaded Programs menu.**

➤You must usually click to run a program.

beside them are programs. You run these by highlighting them and then clicking on them. While a cascaded menu will open automatically when you highlight it, you must click once you have highlighted a program in order to start that program.

Cascaded Menus React In Unexpected Manners
Cascaded menus have an arrow and you naturally expect them to cascade in the direction of the arrow. However, they may cascade in unexpected directions. When there is not enough space to display the new menu in the direction of the arrow, Windows 95 will display the cascaded menu using the opposite direction.

Remember, the steps to running a program are:

1. Click on the Start button.
2. Highlight the Programs option.
3. Highlight the folder containing the program.
4. Click on the icon of the program to be run.

➤Holding the mouse button down can save a lot of clicking in the Start menu.

➤Not all Start menus look the same. You can add options to and remove options from the Start menu.

Alternatively, if you keep the left mouse button pressed as you work through the cascaded menus, you can simply release the mouse button to run a highlighted program. This shortcut can save you a lot of clicking.

There are seven options on a typical Start button. They are:

- *Programs.* As described above, you use this option to run your programs.
- *Documents.* Windows 95 remembers the data files you have worked with recently. This option starts the

appropriate program with your document already loaded.

- *Settings.* The programs here allow you to control how Windows 95 operates.
- *Find.* This option lets you hunt for files and folders.
- *Help.* This runs the help program to assist you with Windows 95.
- *Run.* This lets you type in the name of a program to be run.
- *Shut Down.* This gets Windows 95 ready for you to turn the computer off or reboot. This option was discussed back in Chapter 1.

►*Always use the Start menu to shut down Windows 95 before turning off your computer.*

When you install various programs, they can add items to your Start menu. In addition, you can add your favorite programs to the Start menu so you do not have to work through the Programs option to run them.

Dealing with Menus Other than the Start Menu

Menus, like the ones for the Paint program in Figure 2–4, are used to select actions to perform.

These menus are pull-down menus. They are typically at the top of a program, just below the titlebar. When you click on a menu title, such as "File," another menu appears below the menu option you selected. This is why they are called pull-down menus. You then make your selection from that list by clicking on the menu action you wish to execute. Figure 2–5 shows the File menu from the Paint program.

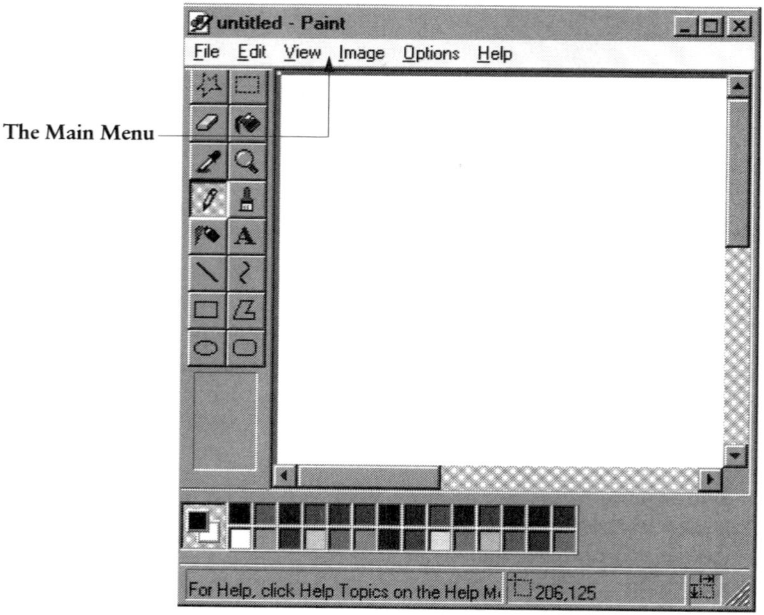

Figure 2–4: **The main menu in the Paint program.**

➤*An ellipsis means Windows 95 will need more information.*

Some of the menu options in Figure 2–5 have ellipses (...) after their names. This indicates that Windows 95 will ask you for more information before being able to complete those actions. While there is not one in Figure 2–5, some menu options will have arrows beside them. This indicates that Windows 95 will bring up cascaded submenus when you select these menu options. Windows 95 immediately executes any menu option without an ellipsis or arrow.

Some of the menu options in Figure 2–5 are displayed in a light shade of gray instead of black. These options are said

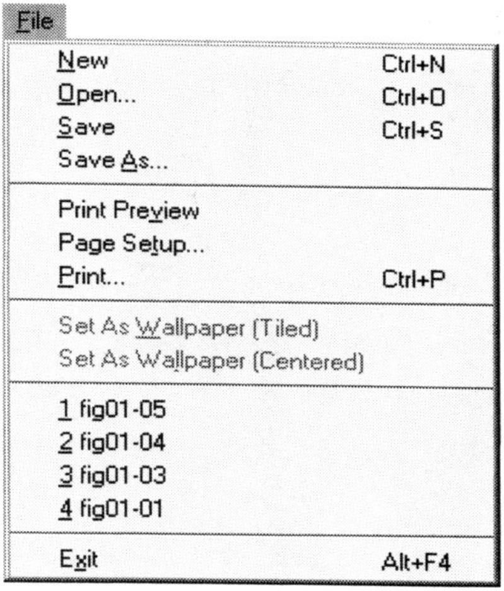

Figure 2–5: **The Paint program displays its File menu. This is a typical Windows 95 menu.**

to be *grayed out*. Windows 95 grays out menu options when it is not appropriate to take those actions at this time. You cannot select a grayed out option.

►When a menu option is gray, you cannot execute that option.

Finally, some of the menu options in Figure 2–5 have keyboard shortcuts displayed after their names. For example, pressing Control–P performs the same action as selecting Print from the File menu. If you prefer to use the keyboard, reviewing the keyboard shortcuts in the menus is a great way to learn how to control Windows 95 using the keyboard.

►Read the menus, they will often tell you their keyboard shortcuts.

►Shortcut menus can save you a lot of time.

In addition to the Start and pull-down menus, Windows 95 uses a third type of menu called a popup menu. Popup menus have two main purposes: as a shortcut and to adjust settings. To display a popup menu, you point to an item and click the right mouse button. The popup menu is then displayed as a "floating" menu. Figure 2–6 shows the popup menu for the My Briefcase program. Once you display a popup menu, you use it just like any other menu.

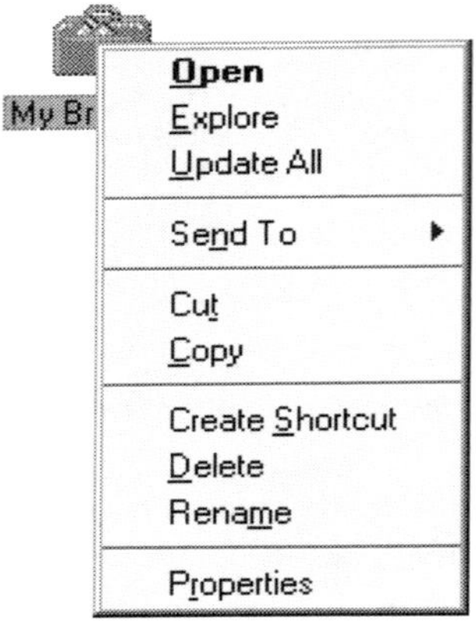

Figure 2–6: **The popup menu for the My Briefcase program.**

Dealing with Long File Names

➤While files and subdirectories get long file names, volume labels are still limited to twelve characters.

Unless you have never used a computer, you know that DOS limits file names to eight characters or less. You might also know that file names can have a three-character extension that you might be able to control. Not only that, there are a host of special characters like spaces that you cannot use in a file name or extension. Subdirectories suffer the same fate.

All of that goes away in Windows 95. Icons and folders can have up to 255 characters in their names, including spaces. As you can imagine, an icon labeled "Letter to Mom about move" makes more sense than one labeled "MOM-MOVE.TXT".

The Long And The Short Of It

In order to be compatible with older programs, Windows 95 gives two names to any folder or icon you create. One is the long file name you give it. The other is an eight-character version that is compatible with DOS and Windows 3.1.

The first six characters of this name are the first six DOS-legal characters from your long name. The last two are "~1". If that is already used, then it uses "~2" and so on. A Windows 95 program will see the long name while an older program will see this short name. If the name you supply is eight characters or less and does not use any characters not allowed by DOS, Windows 95 will not alter the name

Dealing with Icons and Folders

Windows 95 uses icons and folders instead of the files and subdirectories used by DOS. This usage is consistent with its graphical nature.

Icons

Under Windows 95, everything is an icon. This includes printers, data files, your computer, everything. To learn more about an icon, right-click on it. This brings up a quick menu. Select Properties from this quick menu. This brings up a Property Sheet like the one in Figure 2–7. From here, you can view and change the properties of an icon.

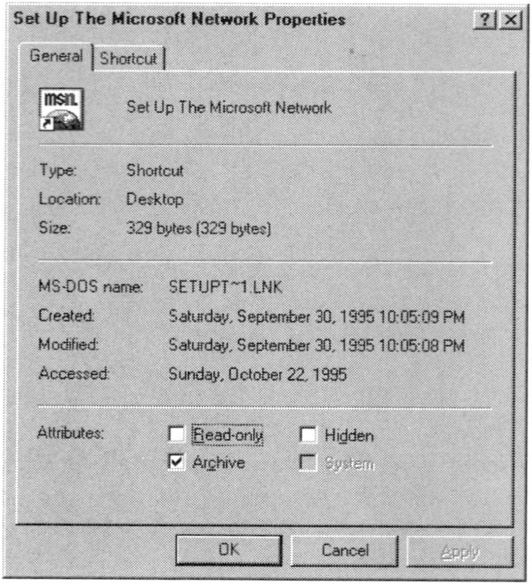

Figure 2–7: **A Property Sheet for the Microsoft Network icon.**

Shortcuts

➤*Shortcuts make it easy to access files and subdirectories from more than one place.*

A shortcut is a pointer to an icon in another location. The shortcut icon will look exactly like the original except it will have an arrow appended to it.

The best way to think about a shortcut is to visualize a file you might frequently use at the office. The normal location of this file is inside a file folder, inside a file drawer, inside a filing cabinet, inside a file room. You could make a copy of the file to keep on your desk but this would waste resources. Instead, you might just have a note on your desktop reminding you where to find the file. A shortcut is like that note, only it will go and get the file for you.

Folders

A manila folder keeps related papers together. A Windows 95 folder keeps related icons and shortcuts together. You can get four different views of a folder:

➤When you see a Windows 95 folder, think of a manila folder.

- *Large icon view.* This shows the large version of the icons in a multicolumn format. The large format is perfect for portable computers and low-resolution monitors. You can see this in Figure 2–8.

➤This view is easy on your eyes.

- *Small icon view.* This shows the small version of the icons, also in a multicolumn format. You can see many more icons; however, they are harder to see. You can see this in Figure 2–9.

➤This view shows you many more icons.

- *List view.* This view is almost identical to small icon view. The only difference, is in list view, the icons are in alphabetical order in rows rather than in columns.
- *Details view.* This view shows the icons one-per-row using the small version of the icons. It also shows the size, type, and modification date for each icon. You can see this in Figure 2–10.

➤This view shows you much more information.

When you get right down to it, there are not many differences between a DOS subdirectory and a Windows 95 folder. However, Windows 95 does so many neat new

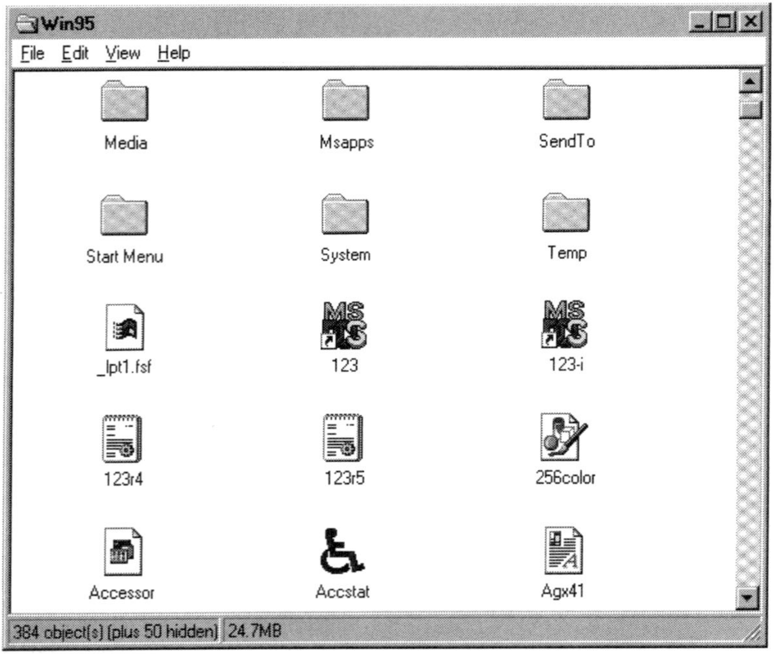

Figure 2–8: **The large icon view lets you see the icons and names on even the hardest to read monitors.**

➤*Folders are just like subdirectories.*

things with folders, it would be a shame to use an old name like subdirectories for them.

Dealing with Windows

Look at Figure 2–10. Notice that there are three buttons in the top right corner of the window. They are shown in Figure 2–11. Every window is going to have these three

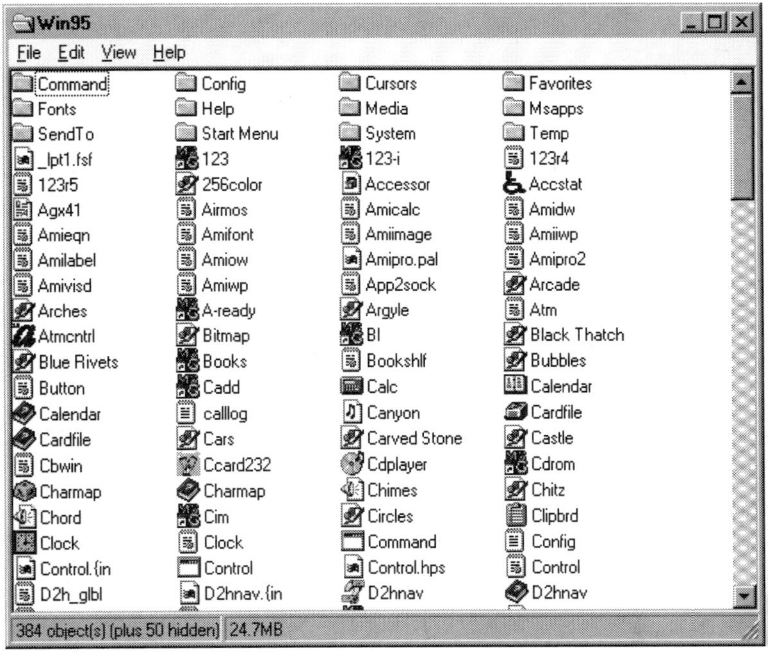

Figure 2–9: **The small icon view allows you to see a lot of icons at once.**

buttons. However, the shape of the center button may change.

➤ *The Restore and Maximize buttons alternate as you use them.*

The Minimize and Maximize buttons are use to control the size of a window. The Minimize button is on the left and the Maximize button is in the center. Click on the Maximize button and a window will expand to fill the entire screen. When you do this, a Restore button will appear in place of the Maximize button. You click on this to return the win-

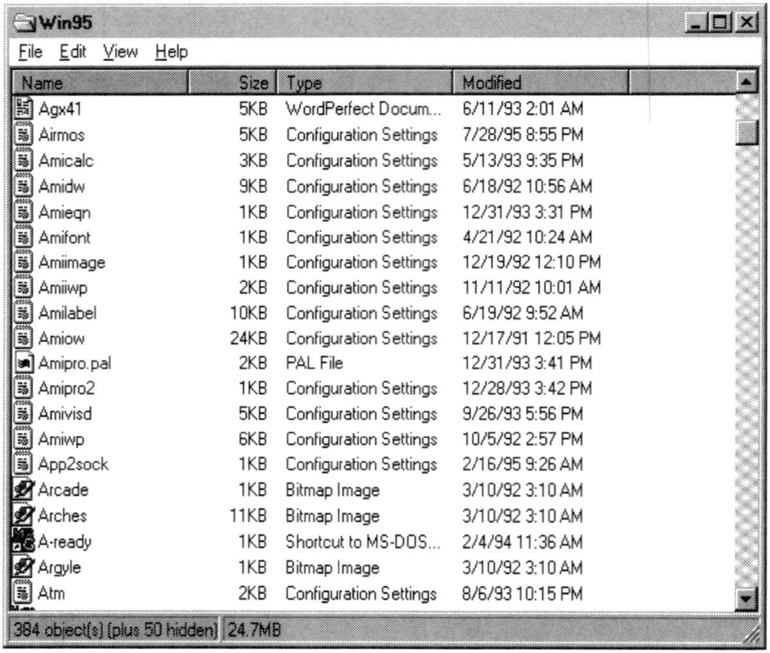

Figure 2–10: **The details view give you a lot of information about each folder and icon.**

dow to its original size. When you click on the Minimize button, the window is removed from the screen; although, it is still in memory. We will see how to switch back to the window later.

The Close button is the button on the right in Figure 2–11. Clicking on this button closes the window. If the window contains a program, it also closes that program. If you have not saved the data in that program, many programs

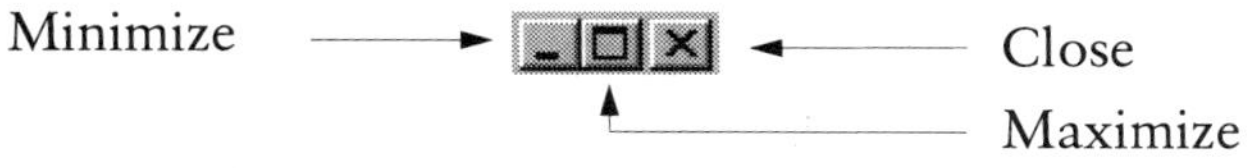

Figure 2–11: **The Minimize, Maximize, and Close buttons. Every window has them.**

will automatically ask you if you want to save the data before closing the window.

►You can make a window any size you want.

The Minimize, Maximize, and Restore buttons are not the only way to control the size of a window. If you move the mouse cursor to any window border, its shape changes to two arrows facing in opposite directions. On the left or right borders they will be facing left and right. On the top and bottom borders they will be facing up and down. In any of the four corners they will be facing diagonally. When the mouse cursor has this shape, you can click and drag the border in either of the two directions indicated by the arrowheads. This gives you precise control over the size of any window.

Dialog Boxes

►Dialog boxes use a variety of methods to get the information they need.

Windows 95 uses dialog boxes to get information from and give information to the user. Figure 2–12 shows the dialog box you get when you print a document using Word for Windows. Each dialog box will have a titlebar at the top and Help (?) and Close (X) buttons at the top right. You cannot change their sizes so they do not have Minimize or Maximize buttons.

Clicking on the Close button is the same as clicking on the Cancel button. Clicking on the Help button will bring up

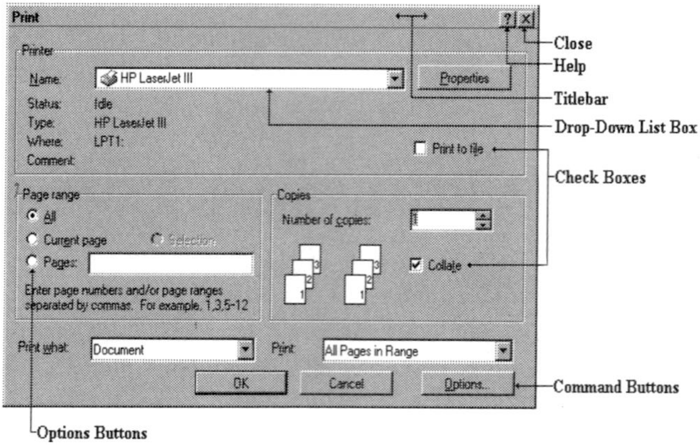

Figure 2–12: **The Word for Windows Print dialog box.**

► *The Close and Cancel buttons do the same thing.*

help for the dialog box. In addition, dialog boxes will have some or all of the following components:

- *Command buttons.* Clicking on a command button carries out the command given as the title of the button. For example, Figure 2–12 has buttons to print (OK), Cancel the printing, and set print Options. If a command button has an ellipsis at the end of its title, clicking on that button will bring up another dialog box.
- *List box.* A list box presents a list of possible choices, and you click on your choice. If there are more choices than will fit on a single screen, there will be a scroll bar on the right side of the list box. The dialog box in Figure 2–12 does not use a list box.

- *Drop-down list box.* This is a single-line list box that displays a standard list box when you click on the down arrow on the right side of the drop-down list box. If there is more information than will fit in the available area, a scroll bar will be displayed. When you move on to the next element of the dialog box, the drop-down list box contracts back to a single line. Figure 2–12 uses drop-down list boxes to select the printer to use and what to print.
- *Text box.* A text box allows you to type in text to give Windows 95 additional information. For example, Figure 2–12 uses a text box to allow you to enter the numbers of the pages to print.

➤*Text boxes let you enter any information you like.*

- *Linked text box.* A linked text box is identical to a text box but when you click on a file name in a list box, that name is automatically entered in the text box. Once you have text in the linked text box, you can edit that text just like in a text box. The dialog box in Figure 2–12 does not have a linked text box.
- *Option buttons.* These present you with a list of options from which you pick one by clicking on it. In Figure 2–12, the dialog box uses option buttons to select between printing the entire file, the highlighted section, or certain pages. You can only select one option and clicking on a new option deselects the currently selected option.

➤*Option buttons only let you make a single selection.*

- *Check boxes.* Check boxes are used to present one or several unrelated options. Clicking on a check box places a check mark in it, selecting that option. Clicking on it again deselects the option. Figure 2–12 shows two check boxes, one to print to a file rather than the printer and another to collate multiple copies.

Conclusion

You now know how to start a program, use the menus in Windows 95 and the program, and manage the window in which the program is running. You also know how to use any dialog boxes the program might display.

CHAPTER 3

Working with Programs

Naturally, the first thing you must do in order to run a program is to start it. This is sometimes called *launching* the program. We saw how to do that in Chapter 2 when we discussed the Start button and the Start menu.

> *Quick Review On Starting A Program*
> Remember, the steps to launching a program are:
> - Click on the Start button.
> - Highlight the Programs option.
> - Highlight the folder containing the program.
> - Click on the icon of the program to run.

Running Multiple Programs

You can, of course, simply load one program and work with it. However, the real power of Windows 95 is when you want to run more than one program at once. First, we will consider what you would have to do if you needed to work with multiple programs without Windows 95. Under

DOS makes it a major pain to switch between programs.

DOS, you can only run one program at a time. If you are running your word processor and you need to make an entry in your database program, you must take the following steps:

1. Stop using your word processor.
2. Save your file.
3. Exit the program.
4. Start your database program.
5. Make the entry.
6. Save the data file.
7. Exit your database.
8. Restart your word processing program.
9. Reload your document.

As you can imagine, this is a time-consuming process.

Windows 95 makes it a snap to switch between programs.

Most of this is unnecessary under Windows 95, since it allows you to run multiple programs simultaneously. If you had both your word processor and database loaded, the steps would be:

1. Switch to your database program.
2. Make your entry.
3. Save your data.
4. Switch back to your word processor.

As you can imagine, this is much easier.

Under Windows 95, programs continue to run even if you cannot see them.

Figure 3–1 shows Windows 95 with three accessories running. They are Notepad, Phone Dialer, and Paint. In Figure 3–1, notice that all of the titlebars are dark except the titlebar for Phone Dialer. That means

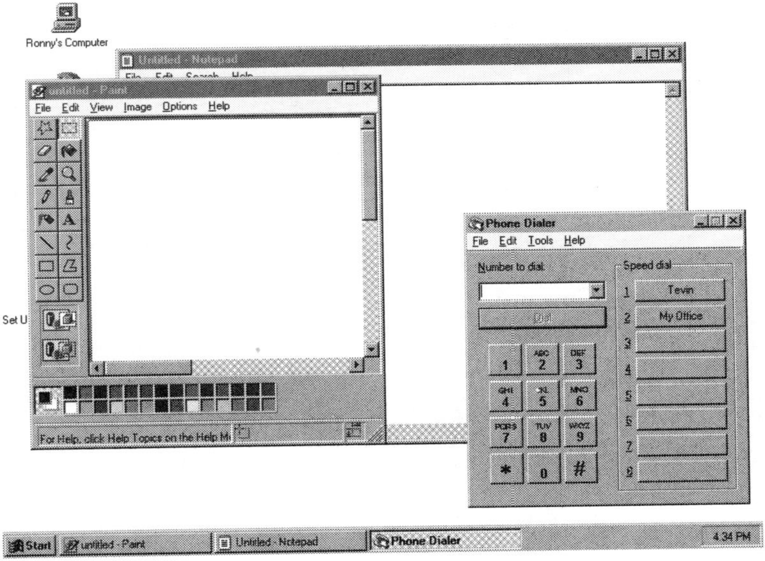

Figure 3–1: **Windows 95 with several accessories running.**

that the Phone Dialer program is the active program. Even though the Phone Dialer is the active program, other programs can continue to run in the background. For example, a clock program would continue to display the correct time and a word processor could continue to print.

The ability of Windows 95 to continue running one program in the background while another program is active is called *multitasking*. This ability to continue working while a program is running is a major advantage when you have a large

➤*Multitasking lets you work on one thing while the computer does something else.*

➤*Your computer will be slower when multitasking.*

document to print, a large database to sort, or some other activity that is going to take a long time.

Starting more than one Program

At this point, you may be wondering how to start more than one program. It is really very easy. You start the first program normally. To start the second program, you simply use the Start button to launch it without closing the first one. You can continue launching more programs in this fashion until you have all the programs you wish to use loaded, or until you run out of memory.

Switching Between Multiple Programs

Of course, this raises the question of how to switch between the programs. When the programs are small and will all fit on the screen at once, as they do in Figure 3–1, you can switch to another program by simply clicking on it to make it active. When you click on another program, its window will jump to the front and it will become the active program. However, this approach does not work in most realistic situations, since each program will take up most or all of the screen. You still have several other ways to switch between programs.

Program switching is asy with the Taskbar.

The easiest way to switch between programs is to use the taskbar, at the bottom of the screen. Windows 95 automatically adds the name of each program you are running to this taskbar, and you can switch to a different one simply by clicking on its button.

You can also switch rograms using Alt-Tab.

Another way to switch between programs is by holding down the Alt key and repeatedly pressing the Tab key. Each time you press The Tab key, a dialog box displays the name of the next program.

Your Taskbar May Be Different

Windows 95 offers several unique ways to configure the taskbar. Normally, it is at the bottom of the screen. However, you can drag it to the top of the screen or either side and it will stay there. Normally, the taskbar takes up one row. If you routinely switch between lots of programs, you may want to make it larger. To do this, move the mouse cursor to the top of the taskbar. It will change to a double-sided arrow. Once it does that, you can drag the edge of the taskbar and make it as large as you want.

Displaying the taskbar all the time wastes several lines of screen real estate. You can easily configure Windows 95 to have all the utility of the taskbar without giving up any screen space. Right-click on a blank area of the taskbar to bring up its popup menu. Select Properties. From the property sheet that appears, select "Auto Hide." This will cause the taskbar to disappear after you use it but then automatically reappear when you move the mouse cursor to the bottom of the screen. Now you see it, and now you don't.

Once you find the program you want to load, release the Alt key and the program loads into memory. You should hold down the Alt key continually until you reach the program you want to switch to, in order to prevent switching to extra programs.

A Quick Tour of Windows 95 Programs

Now that you have seen how to run programs, we will quickly review the programs that come with Windows 95. They are:

➤*These programs are covered in detail in chapters 4 and 5.*

- *Calculator.* This small program lets you perform simple calculations using an on-screen calculator.

- *CD Player.* If you have a CD player built into your computer, this program lets you play music on it.
- *Character Map.* This program lets you display special characters in each of your fonts. If you find one you like, you can copy it to the clipboard for use in other programs.
- *Clipboard Viewer.* This program lets you view the contents of your clipboard.
- *FreeCell.* This is a solo card game. There is supposed to be a way to win every game.
- *Hearts.* This is a computerized version of the Hearts card game. You can play with three simulated computer players or with other people across a network.
- *HyperTerminal.* This is a simple communications program for connecting to other computers using a modem.
- *Minesweeper.* This is a game of logic and strategy where you try to click on safe cells while avoiding cells with "mines."
- *Notepad.* This is a simple text editor. It is useful for editing batch files and simple ASCII files but not much more.
- *Paint.* This is a graphics program for editing images. I used Paint to edit all the screen shots you see in this book. It is surprisingly powerful.
- *Phone Dialer.* This program lets you dial your phone using your modem. It can store up to eight numbers for "speed dialing."
-

- *Sound Recorder.* This uses a microphone and sound card to record sounds.
- *WordPad.* This is a fairly advanced text editor. It uses the same file format as Microsoft Word for Windows. For simple writing tasks, it may be all you need.

Each of these programs is described in much more detail in the next chapter.

Conclusion

Windows 95 makes it easy to run one or several programs. It also includes a number of useful programs.

CHAPTER 4

The Windows 95 Productivity Programs

Windows 95 comes with a number of small programs—sometimes called *applets*—to help you perform simple tasks and have fun with your computer. We previewed these programs back in Chapter 3. We will now look at each program in more detail. We will look at the programs that help you get work done, in this chapter.

If any of these Programs is Missing

You may not find all of the programs listed above on your system. If you installed Windows 95 from floppy disks rather than from CD-ROM, then you may not have everything on this list. Otherwise, you likely did not install the program. For example, the Typical installation option does not install the games.

➤The typical installation does not install the Windows 95 games! You must go back and add the games to your system.

To install any of these programs that are missing from your system, rerun the installation program and click on the programs you wish to install. To start, make sure you have your installation CD-ROM disk or diskettes. Then, click on the Start button. Select the Settings menu and then click on the Control Panel. From the Control Panel, double-click on the icon called Add/Remove Programs.

This will bring up a dialog box. From this dialog box, click on the Windows Setup tab to bring up the display shown in Figure 4–1. From here, you can select the programs to be added to your system. The programs discussed in this section are under the Accessories entry.

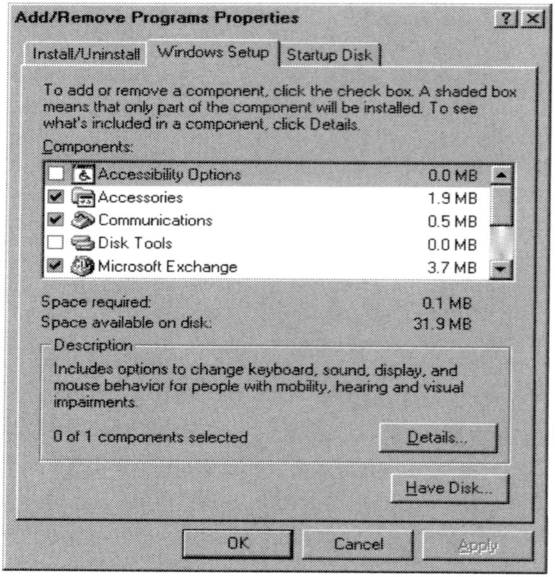

Figure 4–1: **By working through the Control Panel you can add programs to or remove programs from your Windows 95 system.**

If a program has a check mark beside it, that means you have already installed it on your system. If you click to remove the check mark, Windows 95 will remove that program from your system! If the box beside a program is blank, it is not installed on your system. To install it, simply click to add a check mark to that box.

Be Careful With Check Marks
If you remove an existing check mark while trying to install a program, Windows 95 will remove that program from your system. Be very careful if you decide to remove a program.

Once you have selected all the programs you wish to install, click on the OK button in this tab and again when this tab clears to start the installation. The installation program will prompt you for specific disks or for the CD-ROM. Once it finishes, you are ready to start working—or playing.

➤ *Game warning! The Windows 95 games can be very addicting. If this is a work computer, be sure you can control your gaming urges before installing the games.*

Calculator

A spreadsheet is overkill when you need to perform some simple calculations. For this purpose, Windows 95 includes the simple calculator shown in Figure 4–2. It works like a regular calculator, only you press the buttons with the mouse cursor rather than with your fingers. It has a single memory.

- MC. Memory Clear clears the contents of the memory.
- MR. Memory Recall reloads the contents of the memory.
- MS. Memory Store stores the current number in memory, replacing the number—if any-already stored in memory.

- M+. Memory Add adds the current number to the number stored in memory.

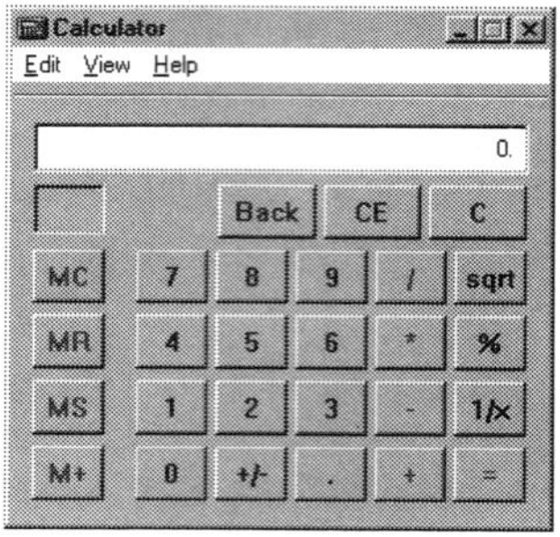

Figure 4–2: **Normally, the Windows 95 Calculator is a basic calculator.**

If you need even more computational power, you can select Scientific from the View menu to bring up the industrial-strength scientific calculator shown in Figure 4–3. You switch back by selecting Standard from the View menu.

> *Adding To The Clipboard*
> The Edit menu of the Calculator lets you copy results to the Clipboard or paste numbers from the Clipboard into the Calculator.

All of the keys on the scientific calculator can be confusing. If you are not sure what a key does, you can click on it with the right mouse button. This will bring up a floating menu with a single option: What's This? You can then left-click on this menu option to get a floating display explaining the function of the key on which you

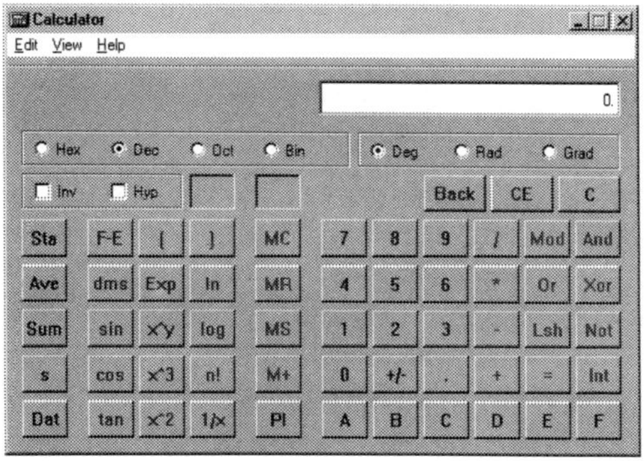

Figure 4–3: **With a single click, the Windows 95 Calculator turns into a powerful scientific calculator.**

right-clicked. Naturally, the Calculator also offers on-line help if you need even more information.

Character Map

Many of your fonts contain very useful special characters. However, finding them and entering them into a program can be a major pain. Character Map makes the process of selecting and using special characters easy.

➤ *The Character Map makes it easy to select special characters you can use to dress up all kinds of Windows 95 documents.*

Once you start Character Map, you will see a display similar to Figure 4–4. Since each font has different special characters, you use the drop-down list at the left top to select the font to display. If you have them, Wingdings, Map Symbols, WP OverflowSet, and WP TypographicSymbols are useful for unusual characters.

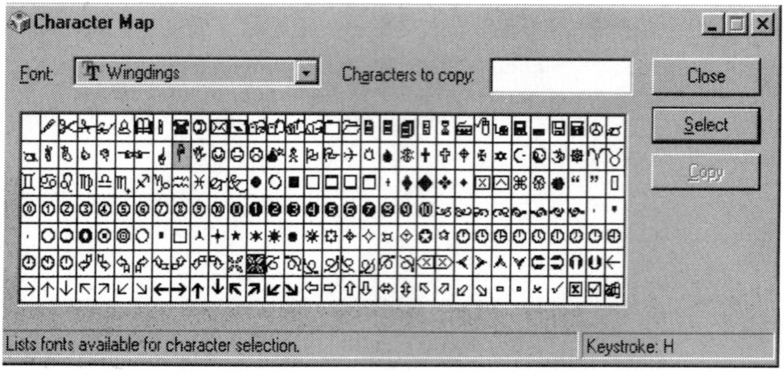

Figure 4–4: **Character Map helps you select and paste special characters available with your different fonts.**

Once you have selected a font, the display area shows all the available characters. If you single-click on a character, Character Map will display an enlarged copy of that character as long as you hold down the left mouse button. You select a character by double-clicking on it or by highlighting it and clicking on the Select button. Selecting a character places it in the Characters to Copy display at the top right. You can place as many different characters in this display as you like. Once you have one or more characters in this area, you click on the Copy button to copy them to the Windows 95 Clipboard. From there, you can paste them into any Windows 95 program.

> *Copying to the Clipboard*
> Copying characters to the Clipboard removes the information already in the Clipboard. Make sure you do not need the Clipboard contents before using the Character Map.

Clipboard Viewer

As described in detail in Chapter 7, the secret to sharing information under Windows 95 is the *Clipboard*. The Clipboard is always active and always available. In order to share information, you must place that information into the Clipboard. The Clipboard can only store one set of information at a time. Once information is in the Clipboard, you can tell other programs to paste that information into their data file.

➤*You do not need to load the Clipboard Viewer to use the Clipboard.*

The Clipboard Viewer lets you view the contents of the Clipboard and exert some control over the contents. The Clipboard Viewer is shown in Figure 4–5. In the screen shown, it contains a sample drawing from the Paint program discussed in the next chapter.

The File menu allows you to save the contents of the Clipboard to a file, load Clipboard files you have saved in the past, and exit the program. The Edit menu allows you to delete the contents of the Clipboard. The Display menu lets you control how the Clipboard Viewer displays information. Since the Clipboard was designed to be a temporary data storage location and works well without the Clipboard Viewer, you will rarely need to use the Clipboard Viewer program.

HyperTerminal

Don't Use HyperTerminal!
Check with the vendor for whatever on-line service you use. Most likely, they have a communications package that has been fine-tuned for their system. These packages are usually cheap, or free, and easier to use than HyperTerminal.

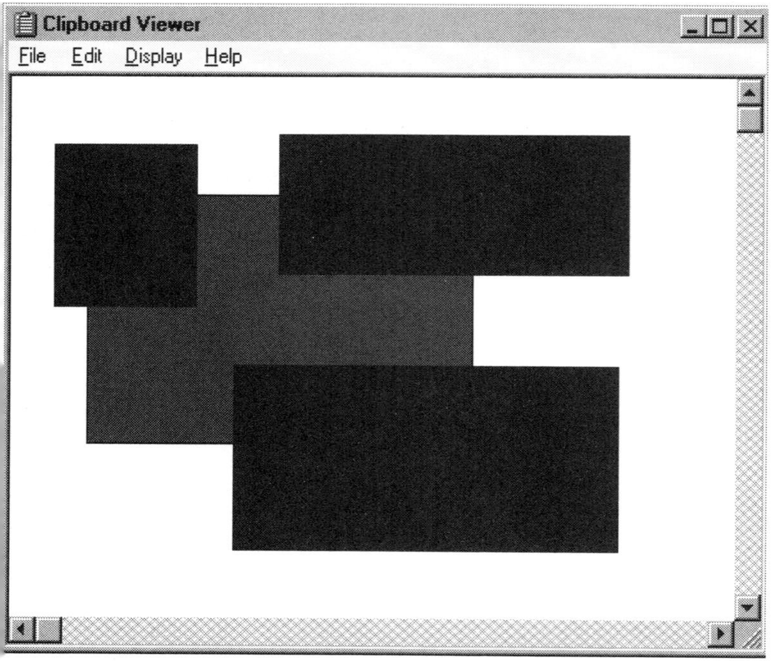

Figure 4–5: **The Clipboard Viewer lets you see the contents of the Windows 95 Clipboard.**

One way that computers talk to one another is over modems connected to the phone line. In addition to a modem, your computer is going to need communications software. If you are connecting to an on-line service like CompuServe or America On-Line, the service will have software you can use to connect to it. This software is especially designed to work only with the service's systems so you get the most powerful connection possible. If you are connecting to the Internet, most likely the access provider you purchased service from can supply you with special software to use the Internet. If you are accessing local bulletin board systems or you have some other specialized need, then you may need to use HyperTerminal.

Configuring HyperTerminal

Using HyperTerminal naturally requires that you have a modem. It also requires you to have already configured Windows 95 to recognize your modem. If your system came with a modem, then most likely the vendor has already taken care of this. If you purchased the modem separately, it should have come with instructions on how to set up everything. Configuring Windows 95 to work with the modem is not hard but it is beyond the scope of this book.

►While setting up your modem is not hard, it is a subject that is beyond the scope of this book.

Before you can use HyperTerminal, you must save a file that contains all the settings that HyperTerminal needs to know to make the call and connect to the system. To do this, use the Start menu, select Programs, then Accessories, and then open the HyperTerminal folder. You will see a screen similar to Figure 4–6. This is just a view of the HyperTerminal folder. Windows 95 creates a few sessions automatically when you install HyperTerminal, and you can create as many more as you need.

To create a new session, double-click on the Hypertrm icon. This runs the Hypertrm wizard. The Hypertrm wizard will first ask you for the name of the session and to pick from a handful of different icons. Next, it needs to know the phone number for the computer you are calling, and it will ask you that using the dialog box in Figure 4–7. This dialog box also allows you to pick the modem to use if you have more than one, and to tell HyperTerminal the country the call is going to.

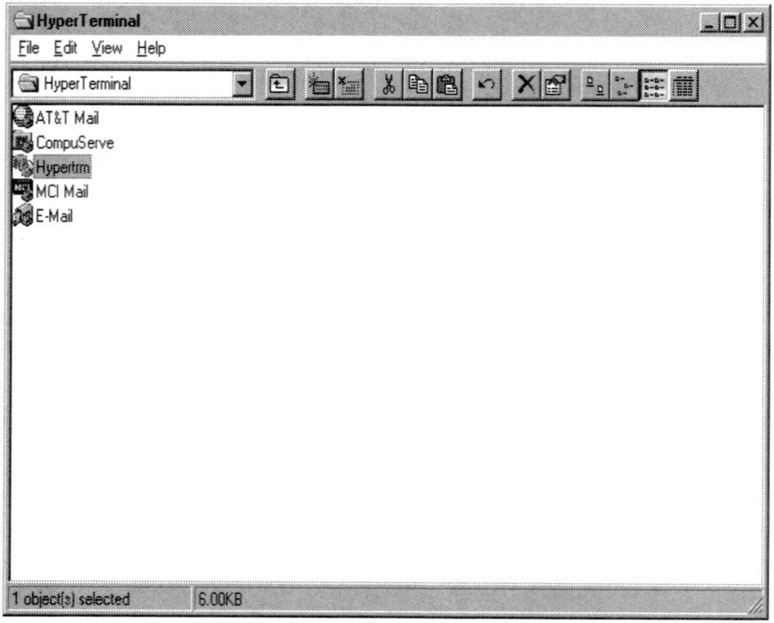

Figure 4–6: **The HyperTerminal folder contains all the sessions you have created.**

> *Calling From Different Locations*
> If you call the same service from multiple locations, you can configure HyperTerminal to have as many different sessions as you need.

HyperTerminal also needs to know where you are calling from, and it will ask using the dialog box in Figure 4–8. It needs to know your location for three reasons. First, the call may be local or long distance depending on your loca-

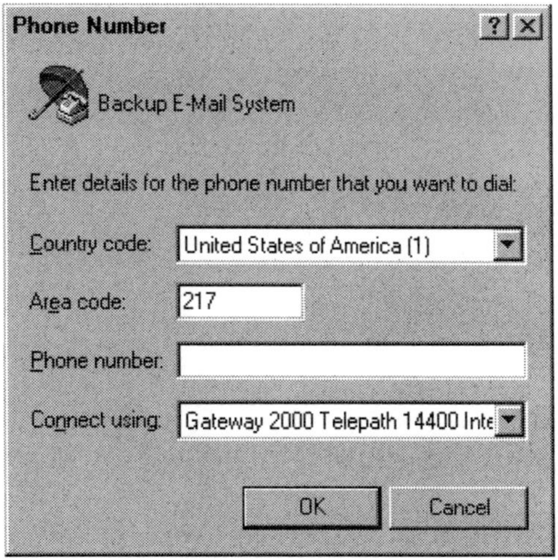

Figure 4–7: **HyperTerminal needs to know the number you are calling.**

tion relative to the receiver. Second, from home you dial nothing to get an outside line, but other locations require various codes to get an outside line. Third, different systems require different combinations of codes and account numbers to dial a long-distance number.

Using HyperTerminal

After creating a new HyperTerminal data file, you can dial the connection directly from Figure 4–8. After that, you can select an existing HyperTerminal data file from Figure 4–6, and HyperTerminal will automatically take you to the dialog box in Figure 4–8 so you can have it connect to that system. Once you connect to another computer, you use HyperTerminal to issue commands to that system.

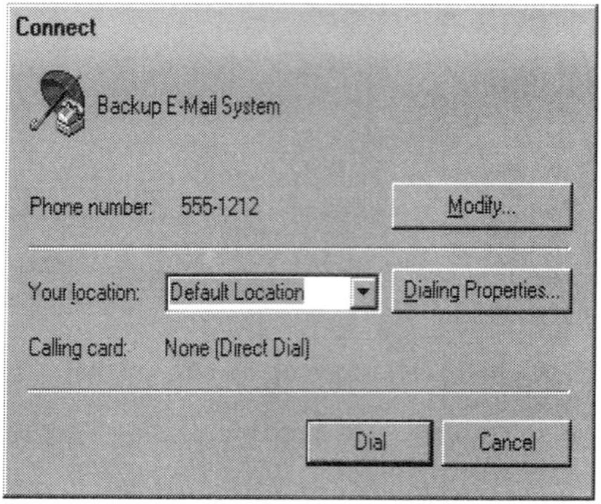

Figure 4–8: **HyperTerminal also needs to know where you are calling from.**

The specific commands that you issue and the things you can do are a function of the system to which you are connected. HyperTerminal can save the contents of all the information it displays on the screen for later review and it can send and receive files.

Notepad

➤*Notepad is great for editing batch files, configuration files, and all sorts of plain text files.*

Notepad is a tiny program designed for taking quick notes and editing small text files. Unlike a large word processor program, it loads quickly even on the slowest computer. In addition to its small size, Notepad will run much faster than your word processor. You can see Notepad in Figure 4–9.

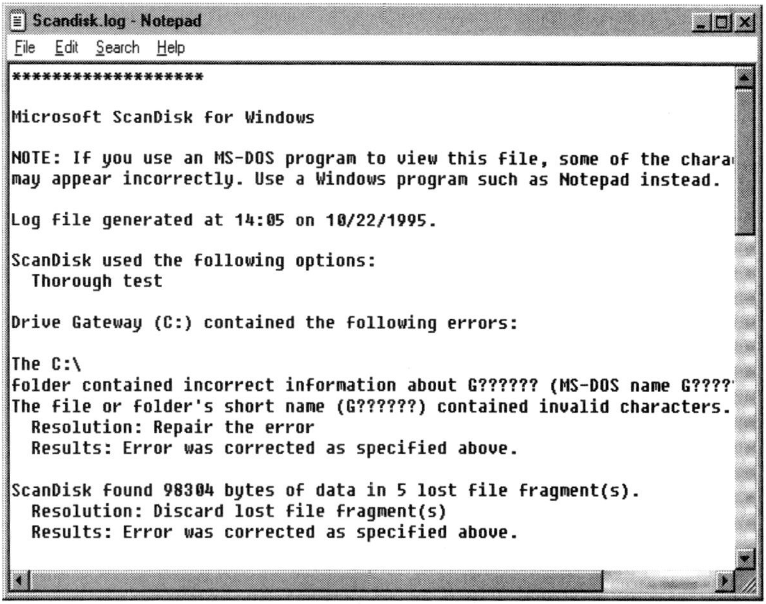

Figure 4–9: **Notepad makes it easy to edit plain text files.**

Notepad offers four menus. The File menu offers the following options:

- *New*. This clears any file currently in memory and starts a new, blank file. Unlike your word processor, Notepad can only work with one file at a time.
- *Open*. This clears any current file from memory and then loads an existing file into memory. Notepad can only edit plain text (ASCII) files.
- *Save*. This saves the current file to disk using its current file name. If the file does not yet have a name, this works the same as Save As.

- *Save As.* This presents you with a dialog box to assign a new name to the current file, and then it saves the file to disk using the new name.
- *Page Setup.* This presents you with a dialog box where you can set margins, change the page orientation, and control the header and footer.
- *Print.* This sends the current file to the printer.
- *Exit.* This closes Notepad. If the current file has been changed since the last time you saved it, Notepad will ask if you wish to save it before exiting.

The Edit menu offers the following options:

- *Undo.* This undoes the last action. Notepad only has one level of undo, so selecting Undo a second time will undo the undo.
- *Cut.* This removes the highlighted text and places it in the Clipboard.
- *Copy.* This copies the highlighted text into the Clipboard without affecting the original copy.
- *Paste.* This takes the text in the Clipboard and places it into the Notepad document at the cursor position without affecting the copy of the text that is in the Clipboard. Notepad can only accept text, so this option will be grayed out if the Clipboard does not contain text.
- *Delete.* This erases the highlighted text.
- *Select All.* This selects all of the text in the document. You would normally do this before copying it to the Clipboard or deleting it.
- *Time/Date.* This places the current time and date into the document at the cursor position.
- *Wordwrap.* This toggles wordwrap on or off.

The Search menu has options to locate text in the file and to repeat the last search. The Help menu has an option to get help, and another to show information about Notepad.

Large Files
Notepad cannot edit large files. If you try to load a file that is too large, Windows 95 will give you the option of loading it into WordPad, which can handle larger files.

Phone Dialer

Using Phone Dialer
In order to use Phone Dialer, your phone line must go into your modem with your telephone connected to the output jack of the modem. This is the "normal" way to connect your modem, so most systems will work with Phone Dialer.

Phone Dialer lets you use your modem to dial your phone. In addition, it lets you store eight commonly used numbers for one-click dialing. After starting Phone Dialer, you will see a screen similar to Figure 4–10.

Figure 4–10: **Phone Dialer makes it easy to dial your phone using a modem.**

To dial one of the ten pre-programmed numbers, simply click on the appropriate button. Phone Dialer will first display a dialog box with two options: Hang Up and Change Options. Hang Up will stop the call, and

Change Options will let you alter the number to call, change your location, and change other options. If you do nothing, in a few seconds Phone Dialer will dial the number. It then displays another dialog box with two options: Talk and Hang Up. Talk disconnects the modem and lets your telephone take over, and Hang Up naturally, hangs up the line.

To dial a number not preprogrammed into one of the eight speed keys, simply type the number by clicking with the mouse on the number pad. Once you have entered the number, click on the Dial button and the call proceeds just as it would using a speed key.

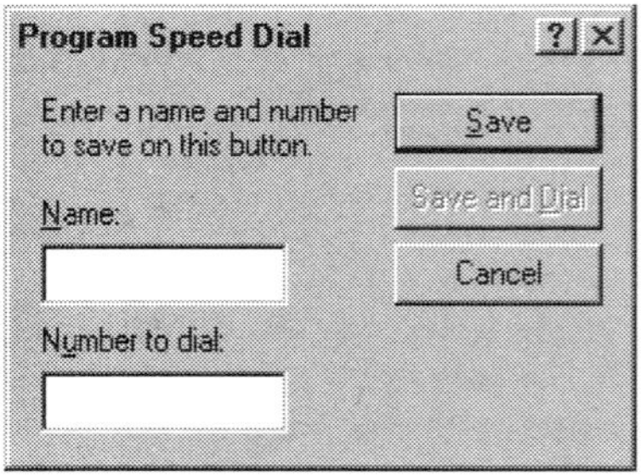

Figure 4–11: **Adding a number to a speed key is as easy as filling out a dialog box.**

To add a number to a speed key, simply click on a blank speed key. This brings up the dialog box shown in Figure 4–11. Here, you enter the name to show up on the speed key and the phone number to dial. You can edit existing speed keys by selecting Speed Dial from the Edit menu. This brings up the dialog box in Figure 4–12 where you can edit the contents of any or all of the speed keys.

You can have Phone Dialer enter more than phone numbers. I program it to enter the passwords for my voice mail and the credit card numbers for long distance calls. Both the * and # keys can be programmed into a call sequence. If you need to delay dialing—to wait for the phone to answer or prompt you for information—just add a comma to the number. Each comma causes Phone Dialer to pause for a few seconds. You can use multiple commas if needed.

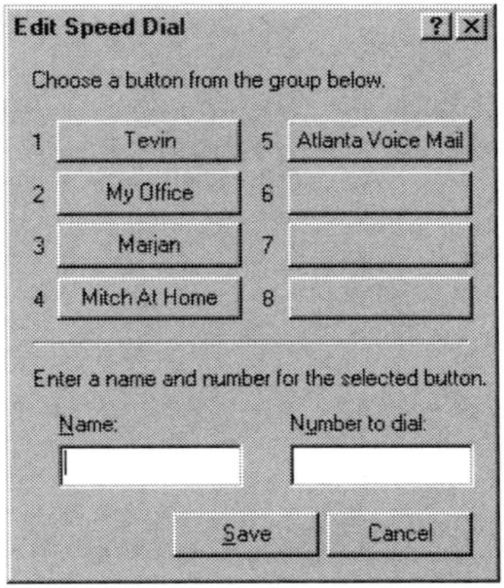

Figure 4–12: **You can also edit existing speed key numbers.**

Tracking Your Time
Phone Dialer tracks the length of calls you make when it dials the number. Lawyers, consultants, and others who bill by the hour can use this feature to track their calls. To see the log, select Show Log from the Tools menu.

WordPad

The most common computerized activity has to be processing words. However, prior to Windows 95, Windows offered very few tools for processing words. There was the very limited Notepad editor discussed above and an underpowered word processor called Write. With Windows 95, Write has been replaced with the much more powerful and

> *WordPad And Your Word Processor*
> WordPad is blazingly fast and tiny compared to modern word processors. If your computer has limited memory, you will find WordPad handy to load and use while working with your spreadsheet or database programs, even if you already have a word processor.

useful WordPad program. While WordPad lacks the features of a full-blown word processor, it does offer enough tools for simple word processing needs. Figure 4–13 shows WordPad being used to write an earlier draft of this chapter.

> *Document Format*
> If you are creating a document that you plan to cut and paste into a word processor, then text is good enough. If you want to format the document and print with WordPad, then select either Word 6, if you use Microsoft Word or Rich Text Format, if you do not use Microsoft Word.

Using the menus

WordPad has six menus. The File menu has these options:

- *New.* This lets you start a new document. WordPad will give you the option of starting a Word 6, Rich Text Format, or straight text document. WordPad can only edit one document at a time.
- *Open.* This opens an existing document.
- *Save.* This saves the current document using its currently assigned name. If the document has not been assigned a name, this option works just like Save As.

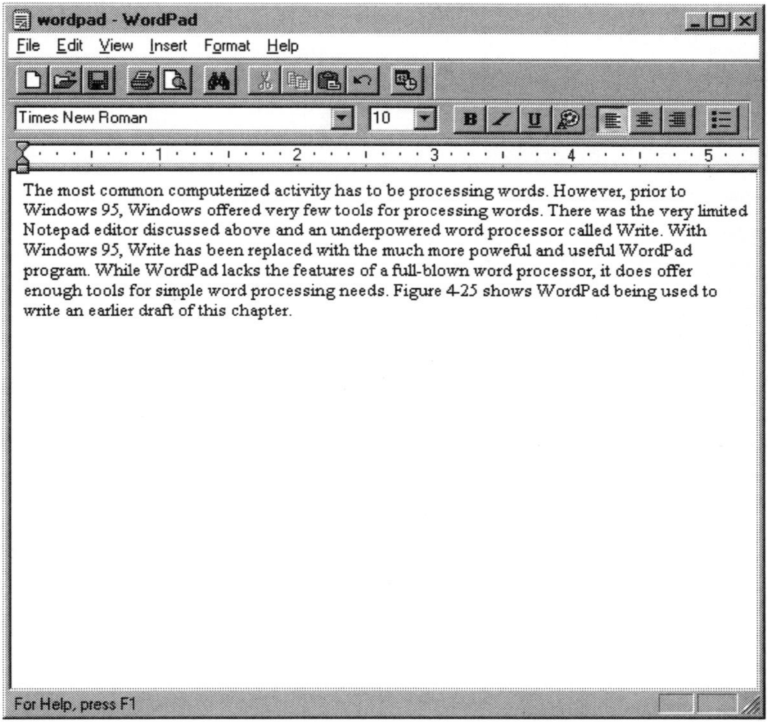

Figure 4–13: **WordPad is a simple but useful word processor.**

- *Save As.* This saves the current document after prompting you for a new name.
- *Print.* This prints the current document.
- *Print Preview.* This shows you what the current document will look like when it is printed.
- *Page Setup.* This lets you control the margins and orientation.

- *Send.* This transmits the document using electronic mail.
- *Exit.* This terminates WordPad. If the current document has been modified since the last time you saved it, this will give you the opportunity to save it before exiting.

In addition, the File menu shows the last four files you have worked on using WordPad. This allows you to reload them with one click.

The Edit menu has options to:

- *Undo.* This reverses your last action. WordPad only maintains one level of undo so you can only undo your last action. Selecting Undo again will simply undo your undo.
- *Cut.* This removes the highlighted information and places it in the Windows Clipboard.
- *Copy.* This places a copy of the highlighted information in the Windows Clipboard without disturbing the original copy.
- *Paste.* This takes a copy of the information in the Windows Clipboard and places it in the document without affecting the copy in the Clipboard.
- *Paste Special.* This takes a copy of the information in the Windows Clipboard and places it in the document with several options.
- *Clear.* This erases the highlighted selection.
- *Select All.* This selects the entire document.
- *Find.* This searches for text in the document.
- *Find Next.* This searches for the next occurrence of text in a document.

- *Replace.* This replaces occurrences of text in a document with other text.
- *Links.* This lets you edit links you have created between this document and other documents.
- *Object Properties.* WordPad supports placing objects created by other programs in its documents. This option allows you to edit the properties of those objects.
- *Object.* This allows you to insert an object created by another program into a WordPad document.

The View menu has options to view the toolbar, format bar, ruler, status bar, and to control wordwrap. The Insert menu gives you two options, inserting the date and time into a document and inserting an object created by another program into the document. The Format menu gives you options to format:

> *My Words Are Disappearing!*
> If your words disappear into the right side of the WordPad window, then you need to use the Options option of the View menu to set wordwrap to "Wrap to window." Now, you will be able to see all of the lines you type. This option does not affect how the document is printed.

- *Font.* This lets you change the font name, size, type, color, and a few attributes.
- *Bullet Style.* This lets you mark a paragraph by using a bullet (like •) or not using a bullet. You cannot control the type of bullet.
- *Paragraph.* This lets you format the indentation and alignment of a paragraph.

- *Tabs.* This allows you to insert tab stops into the document at specified locations.

Naturally, the Help menu has options for getting help about WordPad.

Using the toolbars

➤ *The WordPad toolbars simply give you shortcuts to menu options. They do not add any new features to WordPad.*

WordPad uses two toolbars, the Standard toolbar just below the menu in Figure 4–13 and the Formatting toolbar just above the ruler in Figure 4–13. From left to right, the Standard toolbar has buttons to perform the following tasks:

- Start a new document.
- Open an existing document.
- Save the current document.
- Print the current document.
- Preview how the document will look when printed.
- Find text.
- Cut text from the document.
- Copy text from the document.
- Paste information from the Clipboard.
- Undo the last action.
- Insert the date and time.

From left to right, the Formatting toolbar has options to perform the following formatting actions:

- Change the font of the highlighted text.
- Change the font size of the highlighted text.
- Make the highlighted text bold.
- Make the highlighted text italic.
- Underline the highlighted text.

- Change the color of the highlighted text.
- Left justify the selected paragraphs.
- Center the selected paragraphs.
- Justify the selected paragraphs.
- Bullet the selected paragraphs.

As you can see, both toolbars simply offer handy shortcuts to features available from the menus.

Conclusion

The programs included with Windows 95 let you begin being productive the minute you get Windows 95 installed.

CHAPTER 5

The Windows 95 Recreational Programs

In addition to the productivity applets covered in Chapter 4, Windows 95 includes a number of recreational programs. These are covered in this chapter.

CD Player

If the CD-ROM player in your computer is connected to your sound card, then you can put a music CD-ROM in the drive and have it play over the computer speakers. Many CD-ROM players include a program to play music, but you do not need it under Windows 95.

> *No Sound Card*
> You may be able to play music over your computer CD-ROM drive without a sound card. If it has an external headphone jack, you can plug *external speakers into the headphone jack and listen that way.*

Normally, when you insert a music CD-ROM, Windows 95 automatically loads the CD Player program shown in Figure 5–1 and starts playing the disc. If Windows 95 fails to start CD Player, you can start it manually from the Start menu.

Figure 5–1: **The CD Player lets you play your favorite CDs.**

Much of the display in Figure 5–1 mimics the display on a typical CD player. The large display shows the track number and the length of time it has been playing. The small display on the left at the bottom shows the length of the CD, and the small display on the right at the bottom shows the length of the current track.

Menu

▶ *The View menu allows you to turn off or alter much of the information that CD Player displays.*

The Disc menu gives you options to edit the play list and exit CD Player. The play list is discussed in more detail below. The View menu lets you turn on or off the display of the toolbar, disc/track information, and status bar. For the main display, it lets you switch between showing the time elapsed on the current track, the time remaining on the current track, or the time remaining on the disc. If your CD-ROM supports it, you can also control the volume from the View menu.

The Options menu lets you play a disc in random order, play a single disc continually, or just play the first few seconds of each track. It also lets you set your preferences. These include stopping the disc when you exit CD Player, showing tool tips, and the length of time it previews each track. Naturally, the Help menu gives you additional information on using CD Player.

Toolbar

►The toolbar allows you to control CD Player quickly and easily.

The toolbar has seven buttons to give you quick access to the more common CD Player functions. From left to right, the toolbar buttons perform the following tasks:

- Edit the play list. This is discussed in more detail below.
- Change the main display to track time elapsed.
- Change the main display to track time remaining.
- Change the main display to disc time remaining.
- Play the disc in random order.
- Play the disc continually.
- Play the first few seconds of each disc.

If you cannot remember what a button on the toolbar does, just point to it with the mouse cursor for a few seconds. When you do, CD Player will display a tool tip to tell you what it does.

Creating a play list

➤Not every song on a disc is a keeper. By creating a play list, you control which songs you hear and in what order.

Alice Cooper is my favorite recording artist. In spite of that, he (yes, he!) has never recorded a single CD where I like every song. For many of his discs, I prefer to play the songs in a different order than they were recorded. With other artists, I rarely listen to more than three or four songs on a disc.

Manually programming my stereo CD player each time I load a disc is a real pain! Fortunately, Windows 95 makes customizing the songs you listen to on a disk and their play order much easier. When it loads a disc, CD Player reads a special code from the disc that uniquely identifies it. That way, it can tell which disc is loaded. If you have entered information on that disc, CD Player uses that information to control how to play the disc.

> Getting The Information
>
> A CD disc does not contain the name of the disc and list of songs coded on it, so you must enter that manually. Come on music industry, use a few bytes of the CD to encode this information. We will all love you for it!

CD Player calls the information you enter on each disc a *play list*. It stores the play list in a file called CDPLAYER.INI in your Windows 95 subdirectory. Once you begin to create play lists for your discs, you will want to make sure and back up this file; otherwise, you risk losing all the information in your play list.

To create a play list, you must insert the disc. It does not have to be playing, but it does have to be loaded so CD Player can read its special code. Once you have the disc in, select Edit Play List from the Disc menu or click on the left button on the toolbar. This will bring up a display like the one in Figure 5–2.

Don't Lose It!
When creating play lists, be sure to back up the file CDPLAYER.INI in your Windows 95 subdirectory. After all, you do not want to have to reenter all this information if your system has a problem.

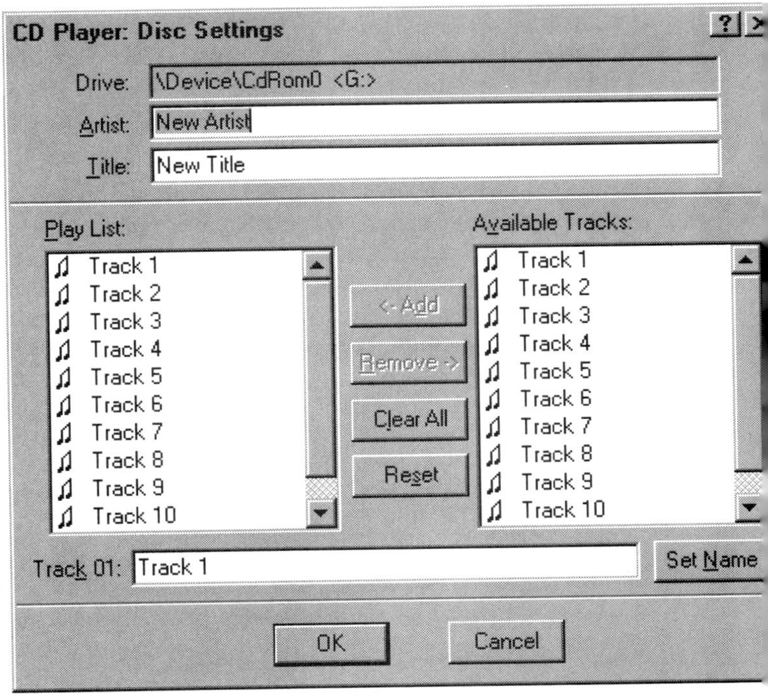

Figure 5–2: **The CD Player lets you edit the play list.**

To enter the artist's name and disc title, simply type over the information at the top. To enter the song titles, highlight the song to enter on the right side, type the title at the bottom, and click on the Set Name button.

Once you have all the information entered, you are ready to control how the songs are played. By default, CD Player plays every song on the disc in the order it was recorded. To remove a song, highlight it and click on the Remove it. This simply removes the song from the play list on the left. You will still have the title you entered and you will still see the information on the right side.

►CD Player can play a song more than once. Simply place the song in your play list more than once.

To add a song, highlight it on the right and click on the Add button. Songs you add are automatically added to the end of the play list. To move a song to another location, click on the song to select it, and then release the mouse button. Once you release the mouse button, click on the highlighted song and without releasing the mouse button, move the song to where you want to place it in the play list.

The Clear All button removes all the songs from the play list. The Reset button returns the play list to its default of playing each song once in the order recorded. Once you are finished, click on the OK button to save the play list. Now, the next time you play the disc, CD Player will use your play list to figure out how to play the songs. Figure 5–3 shows a completed play list.

FreeCell

FreeCell warning! FreeCell can be a very addictive game. Be careful.

FreeCell is a single-player, single-deck card game. In that sense, it is like Solitaire. You can see it in Figure 5–4. Unlike Soli-

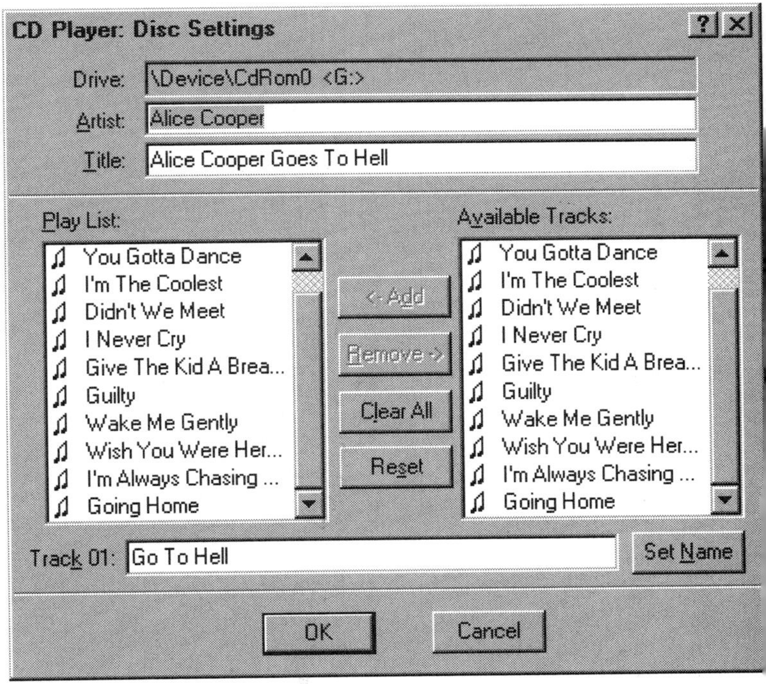

Figure 5–3: **Once you have the song titles entered, you can control which CD plays and in which order.**

taire, there is a way to win every game. At least they tell me that. As you can see from my score in Figure 5–5, I typically lose more games than I win.

When you start, all fifty-two cards are sorted and displayed in eight random stacks at the bottom of the screen. This is the *play area*. Your goal is to stack them in order from Ace to King in the four stacks at the top right of the screen. The

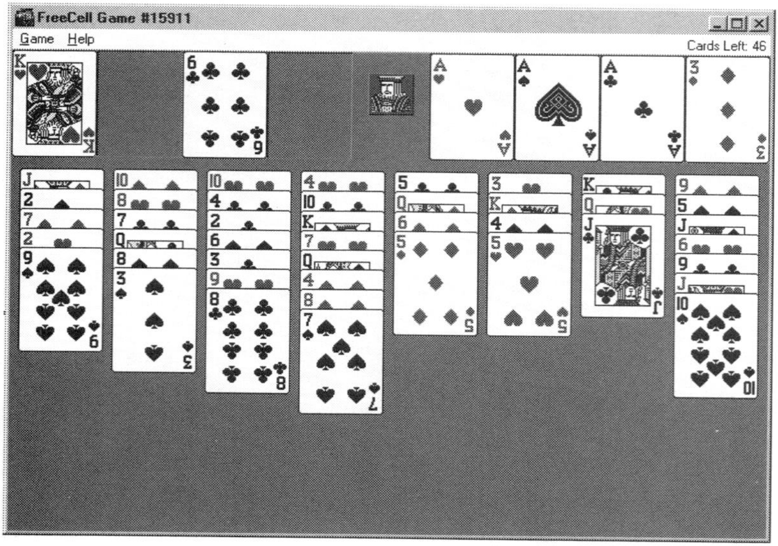

Figure 5–4: **FreeCell is a very addicting single-player game.**

four slots on the left top of the screen are *temporary storage areas,* and you can place one card in each slot.

You play by moving cards around in the play area. Cards must be stacked in declining value and alternating colors, just like Solitaire. Unlike Solitaire, you can move any card onto a blank stack. You can move two or more cards from one position to another as long as every card you move is stacked properly, and you are moving them to an acceptable position. To move more than one card, you must have one fewer empty slot in the temporary storage and play areas than the number of cards you are moving. For example, to move four cards at once, you must have three

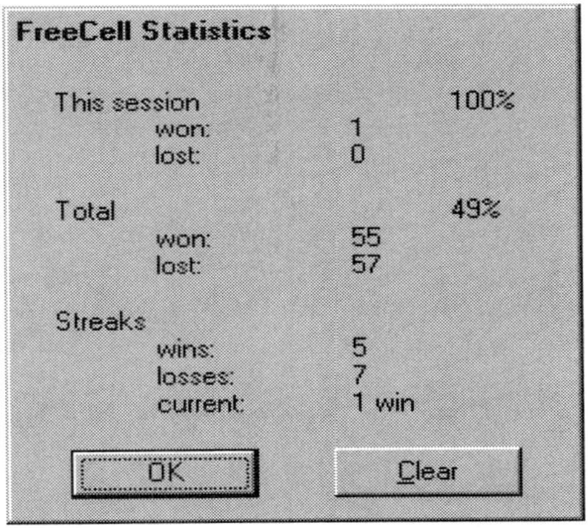

Figure 5–5: **FreeCell will track your score for you.**

empty slots. If you are moving the cards to an empty slot, you cannot count that slot.

The game ends when you get all the cards into the top right slots. Unlike Solitaire, once you move a card into this area, you cannot pull it out and put it back into play. While the rules sound complicated in this description, FreeCell is a simple game to play. However, winning is tough enough to keep you interested.

The Game menu lets you start a new game, restart the current game from the beginning, pick a specific game to play (each one has a number in the titlebar), show the statistics, and undo your last move. Restarting a game counts as a loss so you cannot improve your score by re-doing a game.

➤ *The FreeCell games are quick enough to play often and challenging enough to keep you interested time after time.*

> *Counting Your Games*
> Since the Statistics on the Game menu shows a running total of your games, you should reset the total often if you are playing FreeCell at work!

Hearts

➤*Hearts is a great game for up to four people to play across a network.*

Hearts is a classic card game for four people to play. On the computer, Hearts allows you to play alone with the computer playing all three other hands or from one to three friends can join you and play across a network.

To start the game, select Hearts from the Start menu, click on the radio button labeled "I want to be the dealer," and then click on OK. If you are using a standalone machine, Hearts will start and you will reach the screen shown in Figure 5–6. If you are connected to a network, you will see a blank Hearts desktop as the system waits to see who else on the network wants to play. If you want to play alone or if you have as many people as will play, press F2 to start the game. If you do not have four people, the computer will play the remaining hands.

You begin by selecting three cards to another player. First, you pass left, then right, then across, then you do not pass, and then you start the sequence over again. The object of passing cards is to get rid of cards that will hurt your hand. If you have three or fewer cards in one suit, you may wish to get rid of all the cards in that suit.

➤*Like golf, in Hearts the lowest score wins.*

Normally, the object of the game is to take as few hearts as possible, and avoid taking the Queen of Spades. Hearts count one point each, and the Queen of Spades counts thirteen points. The game

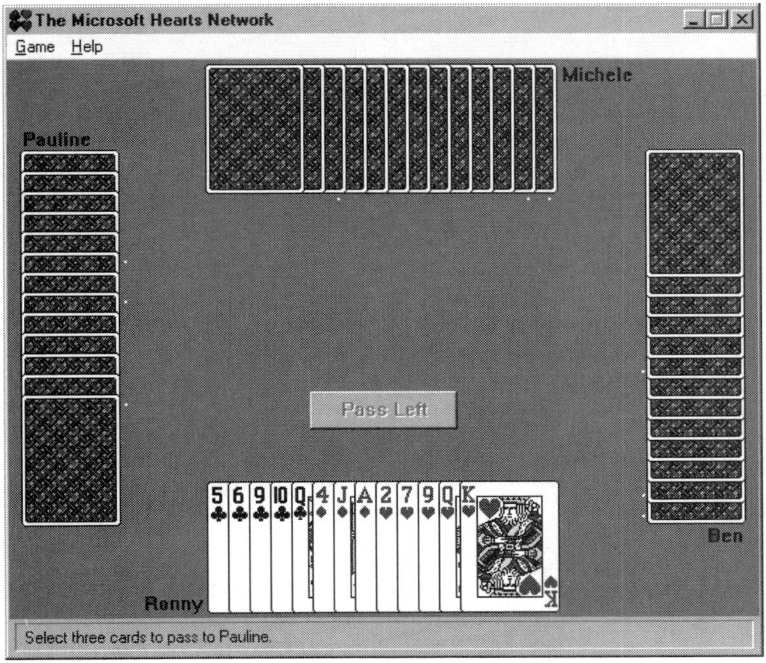

Figure 5–6: **When playing Hearts, you dont want to take the Queen of Spades or a heart.**

ends when someone goes over one hundred and the person with the lowest score wins. There is one exception to this rule. If you can take all thirteen hearts and the Queen of Spades, you get a zero score for that hand and everyone else gets 26 points.

Play begins by whoever has the Two of Spades playing that card, and continues in a clockwise direction. The person who plays the highest card in the suit that began each hand takes all four cards that were played in that hand and decides who leads off the next hand. There are no wild cards. If you do not have any cards in the suit that lead off, you may play any card in your hand. The only exception to this rule is you may not play a point card on the first hand.

If you have the Queen of Spades or a lot of hearts, you typically want to pass all the cards of one other suit so you can play off these cards early in the game—especially the Queen of Spades. Spades tend to get played a lot early on as the other players try to draw out the Queen of Spades, so if you are holding it you also want to keep all the lower spades so you are not forced to play the Queen and have to keep it yourself.

The Game menu will let you set a few play options, control the names the computer uses for the hands it plays, and turn the sound on and off.

Minesweeper

➤*Not only does Minesweeper test your luck, it also tests your logic.*

The object of Minesweeper is to mark all the squares containing mines while clicking on all the squares that do not contain a mine. It looks and sounds easy, but it can give you quite a bit of a mental workout.

You can see a picture of a game that is about half done in Figure 5–7.

At the beginning of a game, it is all guesswork. Anytime you left-click on a square containing a mine, you get "blown up," and the game is over. When this happens, the smiley face in Figure 5–7 turns into a frowny face. You can then click on the frowny face to start a new game.

If the square you left-click on does not contain a mine, then it displays a number showing the number of mines

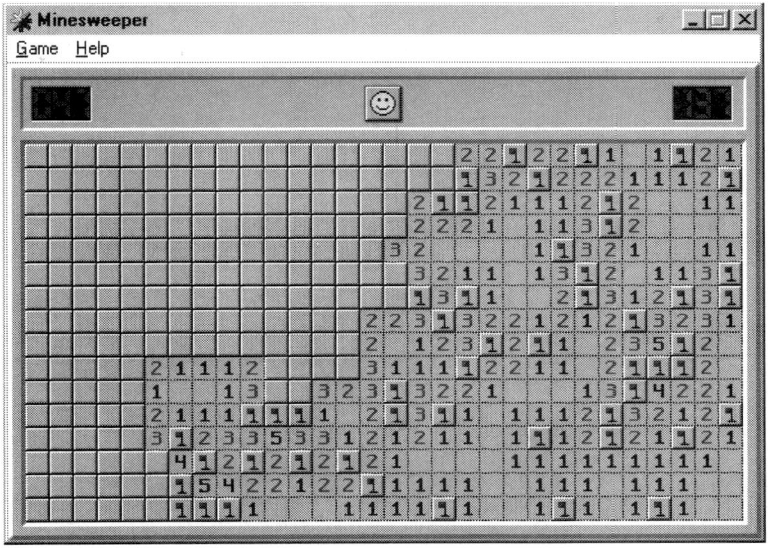

Figure 5–7: **Minesweeper is a game of both luck and logic.**

that are touching that square. If no mines are touching that square, it will turn into a blank square. Sometimes, you will click on a single square and a lot of squares will be displayed without your doing anything. When you click on a square without any mines, Minesweeper will go ahead and clear all the squares touching that square that have no mines touching them.

To mark a square as a mine, you right-click on it. Minesweeper will place a flag on the square like you see in Figure 5–7. If you are not sure, you can right-click twice and Minesweeper will place a question mark on the square. Right-click once more to clear the question mark.

I'm Not Sure
Minesweeper lets you use question marks to mark the squares you are not sure about. After you clear more squares, you may be better able to tell what the original square contains.

When you first start, you naturally have to guess. However, after you click on a few squares, the numbers you reveal will begin to suggest a pattern and logic can take over. After you are well into a game, it is almost all logic and there is very little guessing.

Minesweeper has four different configurations:

- *Beginner.* This is played on an 8x8 grid with 10 mines.
- *Intermediate.* This is played on a 16x16 grid with 40 mines.
- *Advanced.* This is what you see in Figure 5–7 It is played on a 16x30 grid with 99 mines.
- *Custom.* This allows you to specify the amount of rows and columns and the number of mines.

You switch between these using the Game menu. The Game menu also allows you to start a new game, turn off question marks to make the games harder, and see the best times from prior games.

Paint

➤ *The Paint program lets you create moderately complex drawings. It also lets you edit even complex bit mapped files.*

Paint is very useful for drawing simple illustrations. It can also be useful for editing larger bit-mapped drawings. Most of the screen shots in this book were created by pressing Print Screen to put the current screen into the Clipboard, loading Paint, pasting the screen shot in the Clipboard into Paint, and using Paint to select the portion of the screen used in the illustrations. You can see Paint editing a simple drawing in Figure 5–8.

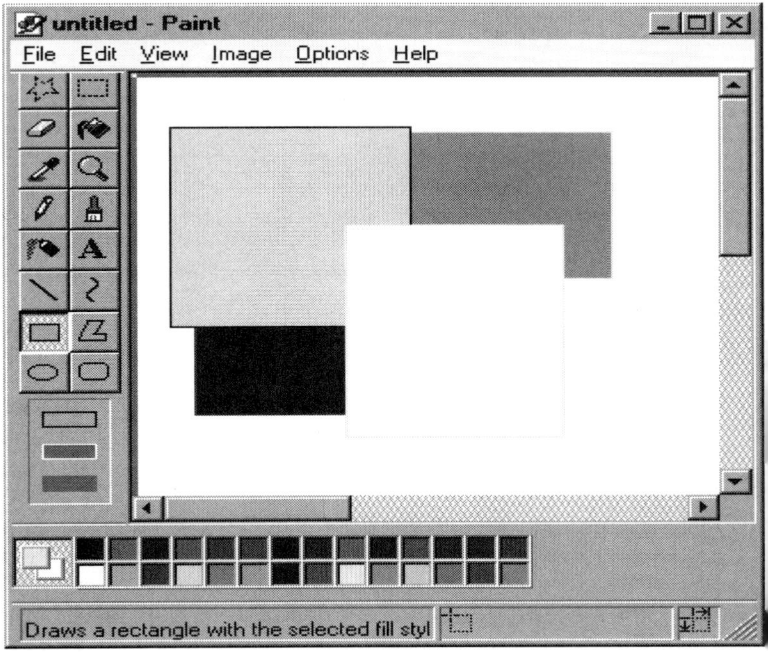

Figure 5–8: **Paint lets you create simple drawings and edit more complex ones.**

Using the Paint tools

Figure 5–9 shows the Paint tools. If you do not see them when you start Paint, check the View menu, as it is possible to turn off the display of the tools. These sixteen tools perform the following functions:

Learning The Tools
After reading these descriptions, the best way to learn to use the Paint tools is to fire up Paint and play with it. Using Paint can be a lot of fun!

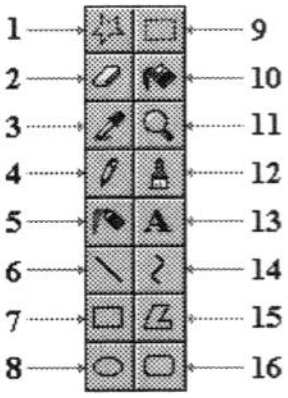

Figure 5–9:
The Paint tools.

1 *Free-Form Selector.* This tool lets you select an area of any shape. Once you have selected an area, you typically copy or cut it to the Clipboard or move it to another location by dragging it.

2 *Eraser.* This erases the part of the drawing you move it over with the left mouse button held down. The area you erase is replaced with the background color. As described below, you select the background color by right-clicking on the color you want. The Eraser will be displayed using the background color.

3 *Pick Color.* This allows you to select your foreground and background colors from the drawing rather than from the color palette at the bottom. To select a foreground color, left-click on the Pick Color tool and then left-click on the color to select. To select a background color, left-click on the Pick Color tool and then right-click on the color to select. Pick Color is useful when you are working on a drawing you did not create with Paint, and it uses a color that is not available from the palette.

4 *Pencil.* You use this to draw freehand. If you zoom the drawing to larger sizes, it also lets you edit the drawing pixel-by-pixel.

5 *Airbrush.* This sprays an area with color. Like a real airbrush, the coverage is not 100 percent on the first pass.

6 *Line.* This draws straight lines of any length.

7 *Rectangle.* This draws a rectangle of any size.

8 *Ellipse.* This draws an ellipse of any size.

9 *Select.* This selects an area like Free-Form Select, only the area it selects is always a rectangle.

10 *Fill With Color.* This fills an enclosed area with color. If you use this on a colored area, it replaces one color with another.

11 *Magnifier.* This zooms in at a specific area of the drawing. Some tools, such as the text tool, are not available when you zoom in. Additionally, you can select several magnification levels using the menu.

12 *Brush.* This colors an area when you click and drag it across the area, just like a paintbrush.

13 *Text.* This lets you add and format text.

14 *Curve.* This draws a straight line that you can then "bend" into curves.

15 *Polygon.* This lets you draw a polygon with as many sides as you like.

16 *Rounded Rectangle.* This draws a rectangle, only with rounded corners.

The best way to learn to use these tools is to play with them.

Moving the Tools

You can move the tools to any edge of the Paint window. To do so, double-click on the area just below the tools without releasing the second click. The tools will change to a thick box that you can drag to a new location.

Using colors

Paint allows you to use two colors at once: the foreground color and the background color. You select colors by clicking on the color you want to use on the palette at the bottom of the Paint screen. You left-click to select the foreground color and right-click to select the background color. As you make your selection, the two rectangles to the left of the palette will change to show the foreground and background colors you have selected.

> *Moving The Palette*
> You can also move the palette. Just single-click above the colors and hold the mouse button down. Now, drag the palette to its new location.

Paint allows you to edit the colors it uses. To do this, select Edit Colors from the Option box. That brings up the dialog box shown in Figure 5–10. Here, you can mix colors and control the hue, saturation, and luminescence to get exactly the color you wish to use.

Using the menus

There are five menus, and you can see them in Figure 5–8. The File menu has options to:

- *New.* This clears any file currently in memory and starts a new, blank file. Paint can only work with one file at a time.
- *Open.* This clears any current drawing from memory and then loads an existing drawing into memory.
- *Save.* This saves the current drawing to disk using its current file name. If the drawing does not yet have a name, this works the same as Save As.

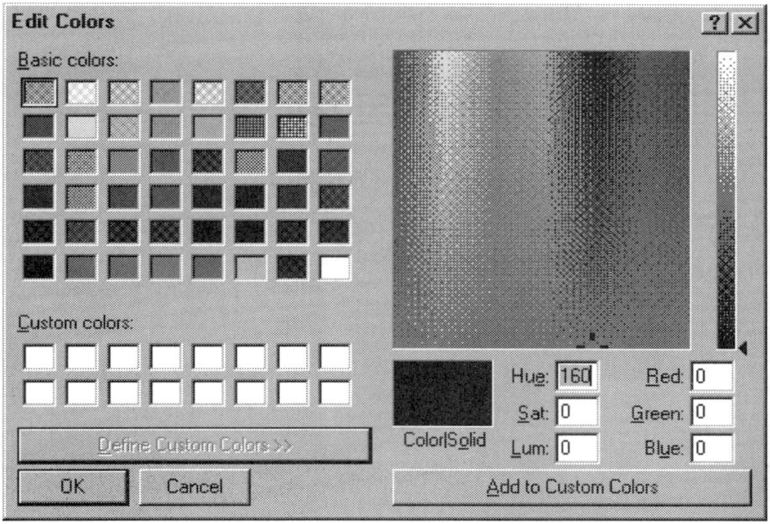

Figure 5–10: **Paint lets you alter the colors it uses.**

- *Save As.* This presents you with a dialog box to assign a new name to the current drawing, and then it saves the file to disk using the new name.
- *Print Preview.* This shows you what the drawing will look like when printed.
- *Page Setup.* This presents you with a dialog box where you can set margins and change the page orientation.
- *Print.* This sends the current file to the printer.
- *Send.* This sends the drawing to someone else using fax or e-mail.
- *Save As Wallpaper (Tiled)* and *Save As Wallpaper (Centered).* These let you turn one of your drawings into wallpaper.

- *Exit*. This closes Notepad. If the current file has been changed since the last time you saved it, Notepad will ask if you wish to save it before exiting.

In addition, the File menu displays the names of the last four drawings you have worked with for fast reloading.

The Edit menu offers the following options:

- *Undo*. This undoes the last action. Paint only has one level of undo, so selecting Undo a second time will undo the undo.
- *Repeat*. This repeats your last action.
- *Cut*. This removes the highlighted text and places it in the Clipboard.
- *Copy*. This copies the highlighted text into the Clipboard without affecting the original copy.
- *Paste*. This takes the text in the Clipboard and places it into the Notepad document at the cursor position without affecting the copy of the text that is in the Clipboard. Notepad can only accept text, so this option will be grayed out if the Clipboard does not contain text.
- *Clear Selection*. This erases the highlighted text.
- *Select All*. This selects all of the text in the document. You would normally do this before copying it to the Clipboard or deleting it.
- *Copy To*. This copies the selected portion of the drawing to another file.
- *Paste From*. This brings in a drawing from another file.

The View menu lets you turn on and off the display of the toolbox, color palette, status bar, and text toolbar. It also lets you see the entire drawing and zoom in at several levels. The Image menu has options to manipulate the images in unusual ways. It can flip, rotate, stretch, skew, and invert the colors. The Image menu also has options to change the attributes (size and color) and clear the image. The Option menu has options to save, reload and edit colors as well as to draw opaque. Naturally, the help menu lets you get help.

Solitaire

> *Solitaire*
> Microsoft included Solitaire with Windows and now Windows 95 to allow people to practice using a mouse. However, Solitaire has turned into the most popular computer game of all time. It is very addictive.

Figure 5–11 shows the beginning of a typical Solitaire game. The object is to move all the cards to the four slots at the top-right of the screen. The first card in each slot must be an ace. The next card in that slot must be a two of the same suit, then a three, and so on. Cards from the pile at the top-left are turned over either one or three at a time, depending on the game's configuration, to help you make moves. In the playing area, you place cards on top of one another in alternating colors and descending order. Only a King can be moved to an empty slot in the playing area.

By selecting Deck from the Game menu, you can select from twelve different playing decks. Three of those decks—the robot, the dealer's arm, and the sun over the palm tree—will show occasional animation while you are playing the game. Selecting a new deck will redeal the game you are currently playing, so do not switch in the middle of a game.

Figure 5–11: **Playing Solitaire can help new Windows 95 users learn to use the mouse.**

When you win a game and get all the cards stacked on top of the aces, Solitaire will reward you with a few seconds of animation. Rather than spoiling the surprise, I will let you find out about this animation for yourself.

Card Animation
You only see the card animation if you are playing a Timed Game. To turn on this option, select Options from the Game menu and make sure there is a check mark beside Timed Game.

Sound Recorder

The Sound Recorder in Figure 5–12 allows you to record your own sounds using your sound card and a microphone. The steps are as follows:

➤Using the Sound Recorder requires a sound card that supports a microphone.

1. Start the Sound Recorder program.
2. Click on the red, round Record button.
3. Record your sounds.
4. Click on the Stop button to stop the Sound Recorder.
5. Use the Effects menu to adjust the quality of the sound. This menu allows you to increase and decrease the volume and speed. It also allows you to add echo and reverse the sound.
6. Select Save from the File when you are finished, to save the sound.

Figure 5–12: **Sound Recorder lets you record sounds using a microphone and a sound card.**

Once you have finished, you can use your new sound clip in any document that supports sounds.

Conclusion

The programs included with Windows 95 let you begin having fun the minute you get Windows 95 installed.

CHAPTER 6

Organizing and Managing your Files

The files inside your computer are just like the papers on your desk. They will continue to pile up unless you take the time to sort them, put them in proper folders, and generally keep them organized. Most of the things you will be doing with computerized files—such as copying them, placing them in folders, and discarding them—are similar to actions you might take with papers on your desk. If you keep this in mind, it will make understanding the concepts in this chapter easier.

Keeping Things Neat

▶*You must keep your hard disk clutter free!*

Remember the old television show called The *Odd Couple*? Oscar was a slob who would throw things everywhere and who would never clean up anything. Felix was a compulsive cleaner who tried to put everything in its place. With computers, you are much better off trying to be like Felix than Oscar.

➤ *To keep your hard disk clutter-free, put up all your icons.*

The key to a neat computer is using folders. You might recall from Chapter 2 that a folder keeps related icons and shortcuts together. Unlike a manila folder, it makes sense to put computerized folders inside each other. For example, if you are working on a project to develop a shopping center, you might create a folder called "East Quincy Shopping Center Project." Inside this folder, you might want to create a folder called "Financial Analysis" for all your number crunching, another called "Approval" for all your correspondence with Quincy City Hall, and another called "Leases" for correspondence with potential stores. If you like, you could place even more folders inside these.

Creating a New Folder Without Explorer

➤ *Creating a new folder is easy.*

When you double-click on a drive or folder icon, you get a window filled with icons. You can view these icons in large icon view, small icon view, list view, and details view. These views were described back in Chapter 2. Large icon view, small icon view, and details view were shown back in Figures 2–8 through 2–10. List view is the same as small icon view, only with the icons sorted differently.

➤ *Select New from the File menu to create a new folder.*

Any of these views allows you to perform simple file maintenance. To create a new folder, just perform the following steps:

1. Double-click on the My Computer icon.
2. If you have more than one drive, double-click on the drive that is to contain the new folder.
3. If you want to create the folder at the root level of this drive, then skip this step. Otherwise, double-click on the folder that you want to contain the new folder. If you wish to create the folder more than one level

deep, continue double-clicking on folders until you open the folder that is to be the home for your new folder.

4. Click on the File menu inside this window and select New. This will bring up a cascaded menu.
5. Select Folder from the cascaded New menu. This will create the new folder and give it a generic name. You can see this in Figure 6–1.
6. At this point, the generic has its name highlighted. If you wish to give it a more meaningful name, just type the new name over the generic name.

➤*Be sure to give your folders memorable names.*

Deleting an existing folder is also easy. Just point to the folder to delete and right-click on it. Then, select Delete from the shortcut menu.

Using Less Windows

As you can see in Figure 6–1, each folder you open also opens another window. If you have to open several folders to reach the one you want, you can end up with a lot of open windows. You can avoid this by configuring Windows 95 to use the same window each time it opens a folder. The steps are:

1. Click on My Computer to open a window.
2. Select Options from the View menu to bring up the Options dialog box.
3. Select the Folder tab. You will see that the top option to "Browse folders using a separate window for each folder" is selected.
4. Click on the bottom option that says "Browse folders by using a single window that changes" as you open each folder.
5. Click on Apply.
6. Click on OK.

You can do this in any window. If you already have multiple windows open, this change will not close those windows. However, Windows 95 displays all additional folders in a common window.

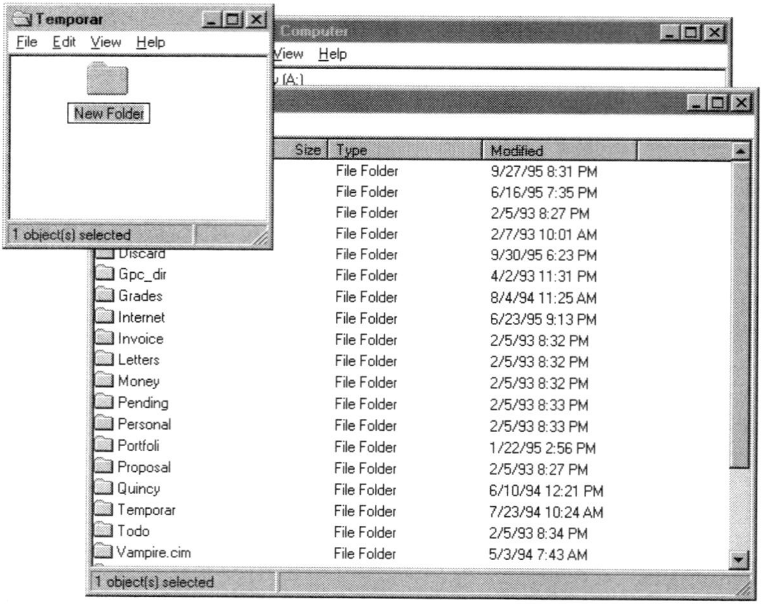

Figure 6–1: **You can create a new folder by selecting New from the File menu in any view.**

Starting Explorer

For simple file management tasks, one of the four views discussed above will be adequate. However, when you need to perform industrial-strength hard disk cleaning, you need the Windows 95 Explorer. To run the Explorer, right-click on the drive or folder icon of interest and select Explorer from the quick menu. This will bring up a display similar to the one in Figure 6–2.

►*Explorer gives you high-powered hard disk management abilities.*

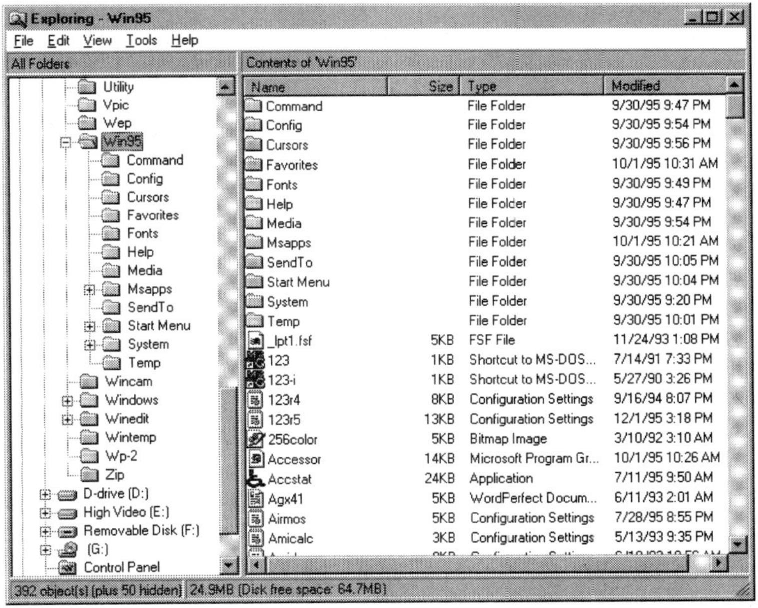

Figure 6–2: **The Explorer window.**

As you can see, Explorer looks just like any other folder in list view on the right side. Like any other folder, you can switch between large icon, small icon, list, and detail views. The left side of the folder shows a list of your drives and folders in an outline view. If you are connected to other computers by a network, it would show those computers as well.

Changing what you see

Notice in Figure 6–2 that the Win95 folder has some folders under it. They are indented from the other folders and have a line connecting them to the Win95 folder.

➤*Pressing the Minus key on the number pad collapses all the folders inside the selected folder.*

These folders are the folders inside the Win95 folder. Notice that the Win95 folder has a negative sign beside it. If you click on the Win95 folder and press the minus key, Explorer will stop displaying the folders that are inside the Win95 folder. They are still there, Explorer is just not showing them. When you do this, the minus sign beside the Win95 folder will change to a plus sign.

➤*Pressing the Plus key on the number pad displays all the folders nested inside the selected folder.*

Notice in Figure 6–2 that the Winedit folder has a plus sign beside it. This indicates it has folders inside it. If you highlight it and press the plus key, Explorer will display these folders. When you do this, the plus sign will change to a minus sign.

For any folder with a plus or minus sign beside it, you can double-click on it to toggle a plus sign to a minus sign or a minus sign to a plus sign. This also changes the display accordingly.

➤*Use Alt-Asterisk to expand all the folders inside the selected folder. Use the Asterisk on the number pad.*

The icons on the right side of the screen show the contents of the folder that is selected on the left side of the screen—Win95 in Figure 6–2. To display the contents of a different folder, simply single-click on that folder on the left side of the screen.

Using Explorer to Manage Files

As you have seen, Explorer is not the only way to manage your files. However, it is the easiest way.

Creating and deleting folders

You create a folder in Explorer just as described above when viewing a drive or folder. You change to the folder that is to contain the new folder, select New from the File menu, and then select Folder from the cascaded menu. You delete an existing folder just as described above. You right-click on the folder to delete and select Delete from the shortcut menu.

Creating files

➤Explorer can create blank files but it cannot start the program.

Normally, you use application programs to create files. However, you can create some blank files using Explorer. Figure 6–3 shows the New cascaded menu for Explorer on my system. Below Folder and Shortcut, you can see the types of blank data files Explorer can create. Some of these are default Windows 95 files, while others were added when I installed Office 95. The data files Explorer can create on your system will likely be different from the list shown in Figure 6–3.

Explorer simply creates a blank file for you. It does not launch the application program and it does not place any data in the file. You can launch the appropriate application and open the file by clicking on the file and selecting Open from the File menu.

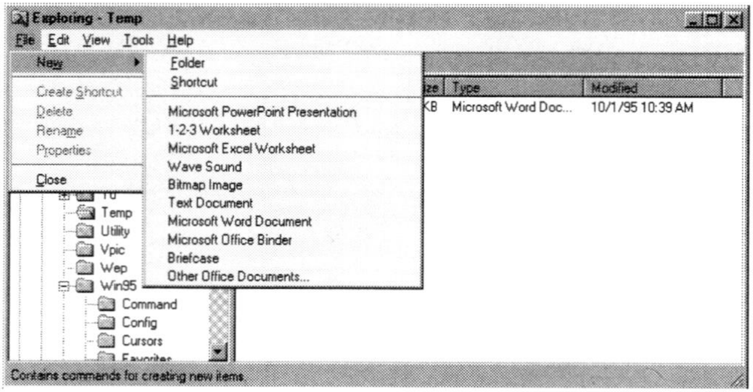

Figure 6–3: **Explorer allows you to create a new data file without launching the applications program.**

Deleting files

You delete a single file using Explorer by right-clicking on the file and selecting Delete from the shortcut menu. You can delete groups of files at once. To do this, you first select all of the files to delete. Once you have selected the files, right-click on any selected file and pick Delete from the shortcut menu.

➤The Control and Shift keys make selecting multiple files easy.

To select more than one file, hold down the Control key and click on each file you wish to select. If the files are all together, you can click on the first file and hold down the Shift key while clicking on the last file to automatically select all the intermediate files. If you wish to select every file in a folder, you can pick Select All from the Edit menu.

Whoops! I deleted the wrong file!

First, don't panic! One of the advantages of using Explorer—or the folder views discussed above—is Windows 95 protects you against accidentally deleting the wrong file.

When you delete a file, folder, or multiple files and folders, Windows 95 hides them so you cannot see them. It also places them in a special holding area called Recycle Bin. You can see the Recycle Bin on the desktop.

►Windows 95 can undo accidental erasures!

To bring back an erased file, double-click on the Restore Bin. This will show a list of the files and folders you have deleted. Figure 6–4 shows this. To bring back a file, right click on the file and select Restore from the shortcut menu. You can also select multiple files and restore them all.

►If hard disk space is tight, watch the Recycle Bin. It can use up a lot of space.

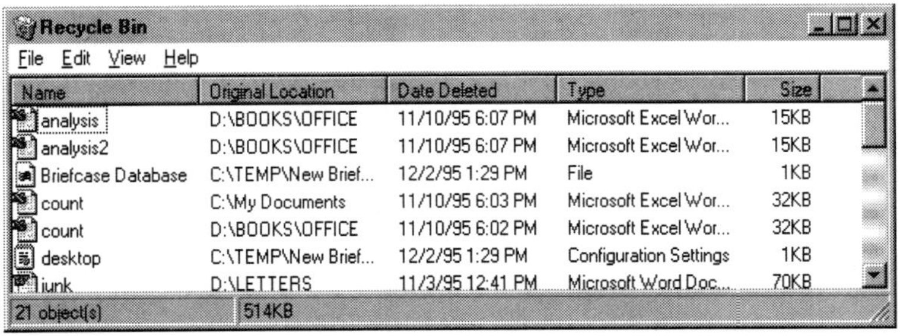

Figure 6–4: **The recycle Bin lets you restore "erased" files and folders.**

All this extra protection comes at a price. Since the files in the Recycle Bin are not really deleted, you cannot use the space they occupy. This is not normally a problem. As the Recycle Bin fills up, Windows 95 will automatically discard the older files. However, you may have to take more drastic measures if you are running out of hard disk space.

►Even if you are environmentally concerned, you occasionally want to toss the contents of the Recycle Bin.

You can permanently erase the files in the Recycle Bin and recover the space they are using by selecting Empty Recycle Bin from the File menu. Once you do this, the files are gone. The space they were using is free but you can no longer use the Recycle Bin to restore those files.

Moving files and folders

Sometimes, you may need to change the location of a file or folder. For example, you might start out creating one folder to contain the files for a project. As the number of files grows, you could decide to subdivide that single folder into logical groups. To do that, you need to move the existing files into the appropriate subfolders.

➤*Drag-and-drop moving is much easier than moving your furniture.*

One way to move files and folders is to drag-and-drop them. The steps to do this are:

1. Arrange Explorer so you can see the file or folder to move and the target folder that is to contain the file or folder after the move.
2. Click on the file or folder to move with the left mouse button, only do not release the button.
3. Move the mouse cursor to the target folder and release the mouse button.

➤*Be careful! Sometimes drag-and-drop moving reacts differently than you expect.*

This approach moves the file or folder to the new location—sometimes!

Using drag-and-drop moving, one of three things will happen:

- *Windows 95 will move the file or folder.* It does this when the target folder is on the same drive and you are not moving a program file.

- *Windows 95 will make a copy of the file or folder while keeping the original.* It does this when the target folder is on a different drive.
- *Windows 95 will create a shortcut to the original file.* It does this when you are trying to move a program file.

Confused? If so, do not blame yourself. Even people who have been using Windows 95 for a long time have problems with this. Fortunately, there is a better way.

For all other drag-and-drop operations, Windows 95 requires you to use the left mouse button. However, for drag-and-drop file operations, Windows 95 also allows you to use the right mouse button. When you right drag-and-drop, Windows 95 displays a menu like the one in Figure 6–5. This allows you to select exactly how Windows 95 reacts.

Figure 6–5: **Right drag-and-dropping lets you decide how Windows 95 reacts.**

As with deleting files and folders, you can select multiple files to move. You select these files just as you would if you were going to delete them.

What is that File?

► *Quick Viewer can show you the contents of many files.*

In managing your files, you may come across a file you cannot remember. One way to see what is in the file is to load the application program. However, loading a large application program to view a file is slow. Windows 95 includes a program called Quick Viewer. To use Quick Viewer, right-click on the file in question. If Windows 95 recognizes the file format, Quick View will appear in the shortcut menu. Select Quick View to view the file. The file will look similar to how it looks in the application program. However, its appearance may be slightly different.

Quick Viewer is only available on the CD ROM version of Windows 95. In addition, Windows 95 does not automatically install Quick Viewer. To install Quick Viewer, insert the Windows 95 CD ROM and follow the instructions. Quick Viewer is under Accessories.

Finding a File

If you cannot remember the location of a file or folder, you can easily find it as long as you remember part of the name. To locate the file or folder, click on the Start menu and select Find. From the cascaded menu, select Files or Folders. This brings up the dialog box shown in Figure 6–6. From here, you can enter as much of the file name as you remember. Once you click on OK, Windows 95 will find all the files matching the name you enter.

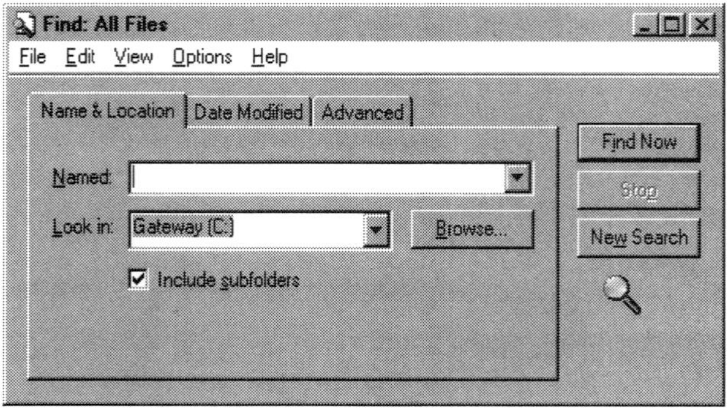

Figure 6–6: **Windows 95 helps you look for files anywhere on your system.**

Wildcards Are Different

If you are used to wildcards under DOS and Windows 3.X, you need to know that the * wildcard works differently under Windows 95. Under DOS and Windows 3.X, the file name *CELL* would match any file. That is because DOS ignores anything after the first * wildcard. Under Windows 95, *CELL* will only match a file with CELL in its name. While this new approach takes some getting used to, it is actually much more powerful and useful than the old approach.

Conclusion

Windows 95 is much more useful if you keep your files and folders neatly arranged. Fortunately, Windows 95 makes it easy to perform necessary file maintenance.

CHAPTER 7

Sharing Information

In addition to allowing you to have more than one program running at once, Windows 95 also makes it easy to share information between programs. This reduces the amount of work you have to do to reuse data.

The Clipboard

The secret to sharing information under Windows 95 is the *Clipboard*. The Clipboard is always active and always available. In order to share information, you must place that information into the Clipboard. The Clipboard can store only one set of information at a time. Once you place the information into the Clipboard, it remains there until you replace it with other information, you manually clear the Clipboard, or you exit Windows 95. Thus, you can place information into the Clipboard while you are in one software program and then later, while in another program, you can use that information.

An Example

By way of demonstration, we will load WordPad and Paint, and reduce the size of their respective windows so that both windows are completely visible at once. We will then draw a small picture in Paint and write some text in WordPad. Figure 7–1 shows Windows 95 with both programs running.

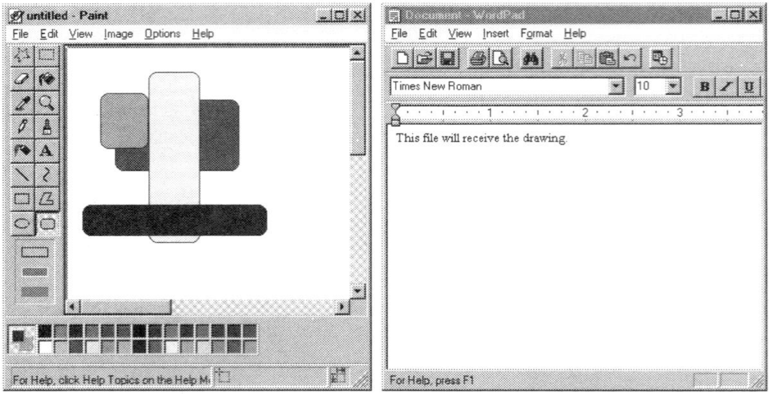

Figure 7–1: **Running Paint and WordPad with information in both.**

Notice that the tool in the top right slot in the Paint tools looks like a square. This is the drawing selection tool. The first step in transferring information is to tell Windows 95 which information you want to transfer and you do this by selecting that information. In Paint you click and drag the mouse so it forms a square around the selection. The process is similar in other programs.

►*Cut and copy place information into the Clipboard.*

The second step is to place the selected information into the Clipboard. You do this using the Edit menu. There are two related options on the Edit menu, Copy and Cut. Copy is like a photocopier: it places an exact copy of the information into the Clipboard without disturbing the original version of the information. Cut also places the information into the Clipboard but it removes the information from the data file. The method you will use depends on what you are trying to accomplish, but you will end up using Copy more than Cut.

►Cut removes the highlighted data. Copy does not.

The final step is to go to the program you want to use to receive the data. Once in that program, place the cursor at the point where you want the information inserted. Finally, select Paste from the Edit menu. This places a copy of the information into the current file at the cursor location. It does not disturb the copy that is in the Clipboard so you can paste the information as many different times as you like at different locations and even in different programs. Figure 7–2 shows the WordPad document with the drawing pasted into it. WordPad accepts the picture even though it is unable to create the picture itself. It will save the picture as part of its data file and will print the picture as part of the document.

►Paste sends a copy of the data in the Clipboard. The copy in the Clipboard is unaffected.

►You use the Clipboard to transfer information between programs.

Clipboard Viewer

Windows 95 includes a program called Clipboard Viewer. Clipboard Viewer lets you view the current contents of the Clipboard. It also lets you save those contents to a file if you want to use them again in another session, reload Clipboard data files for later reuse, and it lets you clear the contents of the Clipboard. Since any new data you place into the Clipboard automatically removes its existing contents, you rarely need the clear option.

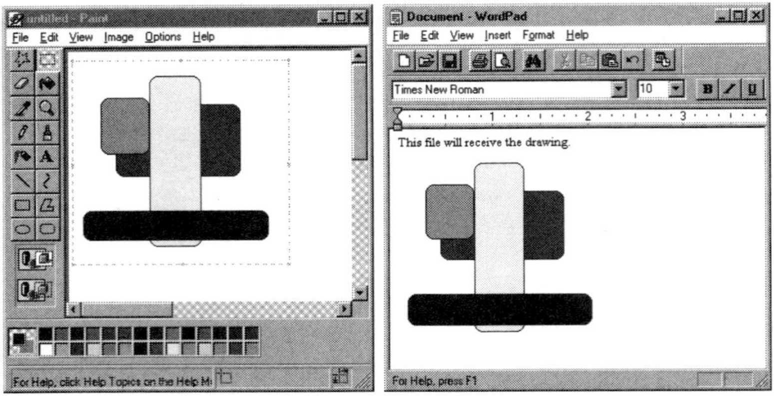

Figure 7–2: **The results after pasting the drawing into WordPad.**

Object Linking and Embedding

➤*Warning: OLE uses a lot of memory.*

In the preceding example, we simply transferred a copy of the data from Paint to WordPad. This means you end up saving two copies of the data, once in the Paint data file and again in the WordPad data file. It also means that if you update the data in the Paint data file, you have to manually transfer the updated version to the WordPad data file.

Object linking and embedding is a method of avoiding the dual problems of keeping two copies of data and having to manually transfer updates. There are two approaches to this and we will look at both of them. By the way, Object linking and embedding is usually referred to by its initials—OLE. This is pronounced *oh-lay,* although many people simply refer to it by the initials.

You should also know that OLE takes a lot of memory to work properly. If your machine has 4 Mb of RAM, you can create simple OLE links. However, Windows 95 will work with these links extremely slowly. OLE links are slow even on a machine with 8 Mb of RAM. To use OLE links effectively, you really need at least 12 Mb of RAM.

Copy and paste review

In the example, we simply copied the data into the Clipboard while in Paint and then pasted the data while in WordPad. The result is one data file containing both text and a drawing. Once we create the WordPad document, there is no connection between that document and the Paint program we used to create the document.

Object linking

Rather than pasting a simple drawing, assume you are pasting stock prices from a spreadsheet program into a report you are writing using a word processor. Since stock quotes frequently change, both the spreadsheet and the report will need to frequently change. However, you want to update the report automatically when the spreadsheet changes.

►Links save space by pointing to the data.

The solution is to not paste the spreadsheet data into the report. Rather, simply paste a pointer (called a link) that tells your word processor where to find the spreadsheet data. That way, every time you update the spreadsheet data, the link in the word processor will automatically load the new data.

The steps are very similar to copy and paste. You highlight the data in the spreadsheet and select Copy from the Edit menu. Next, you position the cursor in the word processing document that is to receive the data. However, you do not select Paste from the Edit menu. Rather, you select Paste Special from the Edit menu. This brings up the dialog box shown in Figure 7–3. From here, select link and Win-

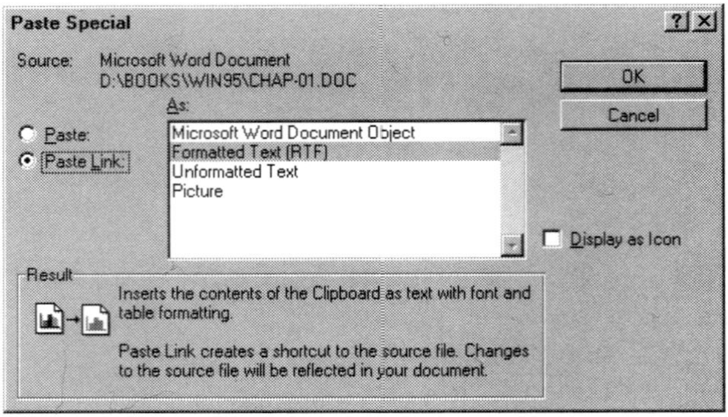

Figure 7–3: **The Paste Special dialog box lets you create links and embed objects.**

dows 95 inserts a link back to the original data. Now, any changes to the original document are reflected in this linked version.

➤*You cannot link everything.*

Note that you cannot create a link for every kind of data that you can paste. For example, you cannot create a link from part of a Paint document into a WordPad document. The only way to be sure is to try it and see if it works.

Object embedding

➤*Embedding puts one file inside another file.*

Now, assume you are using your word processor to write a report and you need to crunch some numbers to go into the report. You could create a separate spreadsheet file and link to it, but that seems wasteful since you will never use the numbers outside the report. The solution is to embed a spreadsheet document inside the word processor document. The word processor will save the resulting spreadsheet as part of its file and you could only access the spreadsheet data from within the word processor; however, the spreadsheet program would actually process the file. In OLE terminology, the word processor data file is called the *container*, the spreadsheet data is called the *embedded object*, and the finished report is called a *compound document*.

To embed an object, select Object from the Insert menu. This brings up the Object dialog box shown in Figure 7–4. From here, you select the type of object to embed in your document. The list of available objects in Figure 7–4 is a function of the different software packages you have installed so your system will have different objects available.

➤*You can embed without first starting the program.*

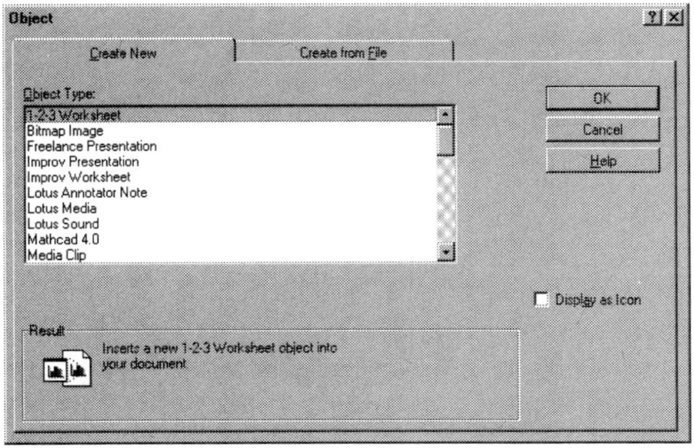

Figure 7–4: **You can embed any type of object available on your system.**

Once you have inserted the object, you double-click on it to edit the object. When you double-click on the object, Windows 95 will load the appropriate program to

➤*Double-clicking lets you edit an embedded object.*

allow you to edit the object. For example, if you embed a Lotus object in a Word document, double-clicking on the object would bring up Lotus to edit the object. You would edit the rest of the document using Word.

What difference does it make?

When you print the resulting document, there is no difference between one created using copy and paste, linking, or embedding. The difference is in how easy it is to update the target file when the source file changes, where the data you are transferring is stored, and how many copies of the data you will save. Each approach makes sense in different situations.

Conclusion

Windows 95 makes it easy to share data between different applications—even if those applications come from different vendors.

CHAPTER 8

Getting Help

On-line help (*help,* for short) is information about a program stored in the computer. Storing it on the computer means you can bring it up and read it while you are using that program. This is often more convenient than software manuals. On-line help is always available while you are using the program, and you do not have to worry about losing it. On-line help is especially useful if you are using a portable computer and do not have the software manual with you.

►With Windows 95, help is always close at hand.

Windows 95 includes a special program for displaying on-line help. Since the Windows 95 help engine handles most of the help system, rather than the individual software programs, on-line help typically looks much the same for all programs. Since most on-line help looks the same, we will use the Paint program as an example.

Starting Help

You can start using the help system by using the Help menu option that is available in most programs. You can also select Help from the Start menu. In many programs, you can also press the F1 key.

Using Help

➤*The help index works just like a book index.*

When you start the help system, you will see three views of the help system. The first view is the Contents tab, shown in Figure 8–1. This is just like the table of contents for this book. It divides the help file into logical groups of topics. The second view is

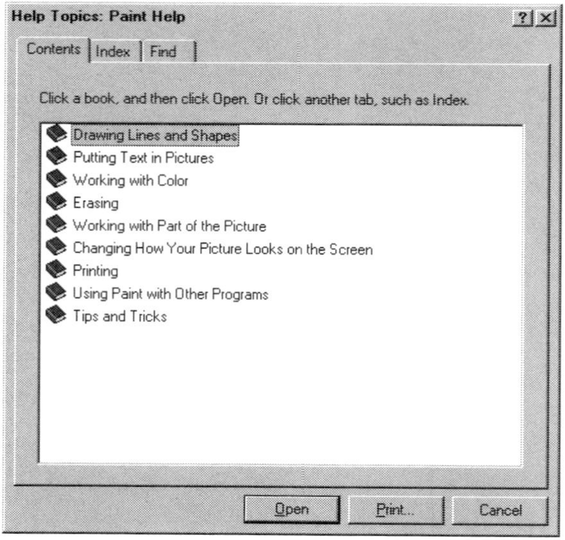

Figure 8–1: **The Contents tab of the Paint help file.**

the Index tab, shown in Figure 8–2. This is just like the index at the back of this book. It allows you to jump directly to topics the indexed considered important. The third view is the Find tab, shown in Figure 8–3. This allows you to search for any word or phrase in the help file. The first time you use this option for each help file, you may have to wait a few minutes while Windows 95 processes the help file.

►Help allows you to search the help file for any word or phrase.

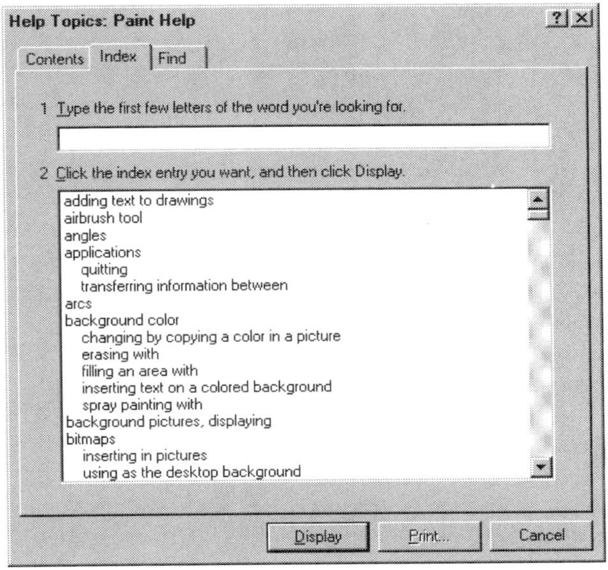

Figure 8–2: **The Index tab of the Paint help file.**

With either of these search methods, you eventually find a help topic you wish to read. Once you have located an interesting topic, you double-click on that topic to read it.

►Getting help is always easy.

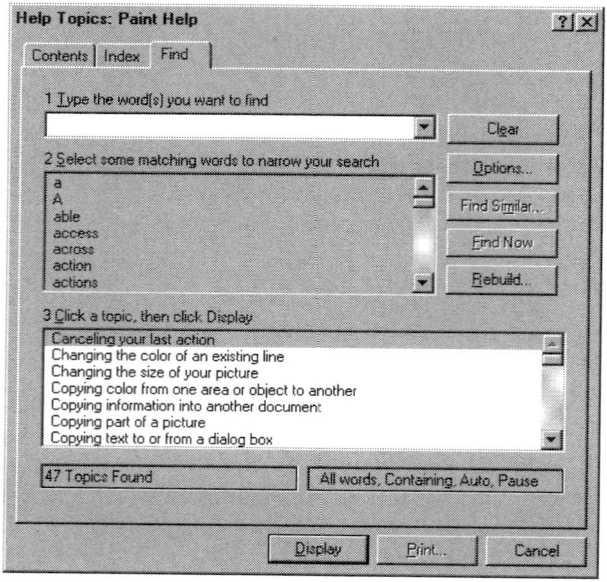

Figure 8–3: **The Find tab lets you search for any word or phrase you like.**

Enhancements

Windows 95 help files offer three types of enhancements:

- *Definitions.* Definitions are shown in a green, broken-underlined font. To view one, move the cursor over the word, and it changes to a hand pointing with a finger. Click on the word, and a definition appears. Once you finish reading the definition, click again or press the Escape key to remove the definition. Definitions only appear the first time the word is used in each topic. Figure 8–4 shows a definition.

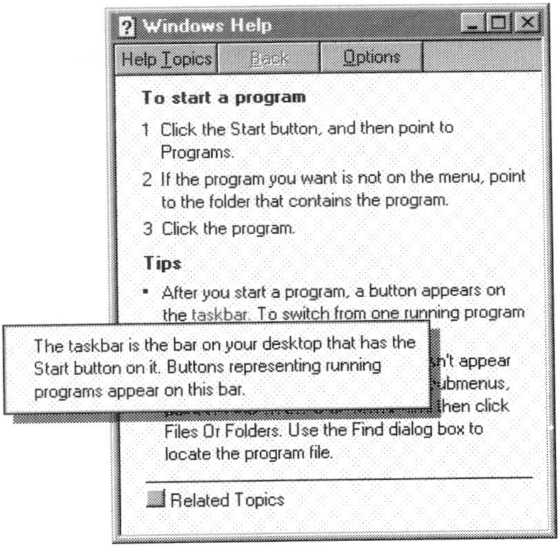

Figure 8–4: **Popup definitions explain unfamiliar terms.**

- *Jump Buttons.* Jump buttons let you quickly jump to another topic or a Windows 95 feature being discussed. You can see this in Figure 8–5.

►*Jump and selection buttons let you see what you want to see.*

- *Selection Buttons.* These list other topics of interest. Once you click on one, it reacts just like a jump button. Figure 8–6 shows this.

Some help displays will include graphic images or even animation to make their points.

Keeping Help Visible

If you are using help to find out how to do something, you do not have to take notes. Just click on the Option button

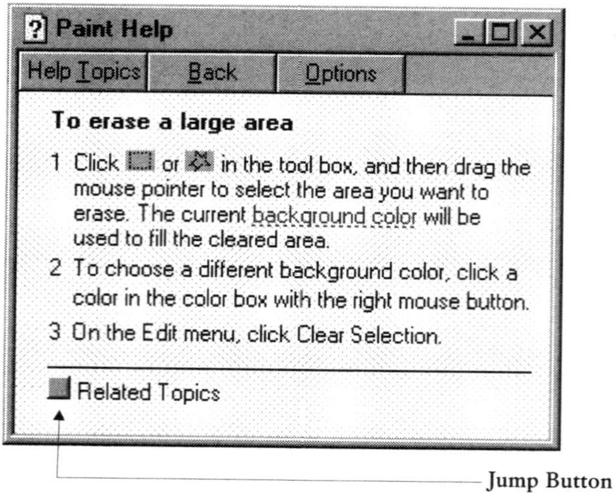

Figure 8–5: **Jump buttons let you quickly move to other topics or features.**

and select Keep Help On Top, and you can keep the help file on top of your work until you close it. This makes following along much easier.

Taking Notes

If you learn something while working through the help system that you want to write down, you can save that comment with the help system so it will be handy the next time you use help. To do this, select Annotate from the Option button. This will bring up a small note area where you can enter and save your notes. Later, the same process will allow you to review these notes.

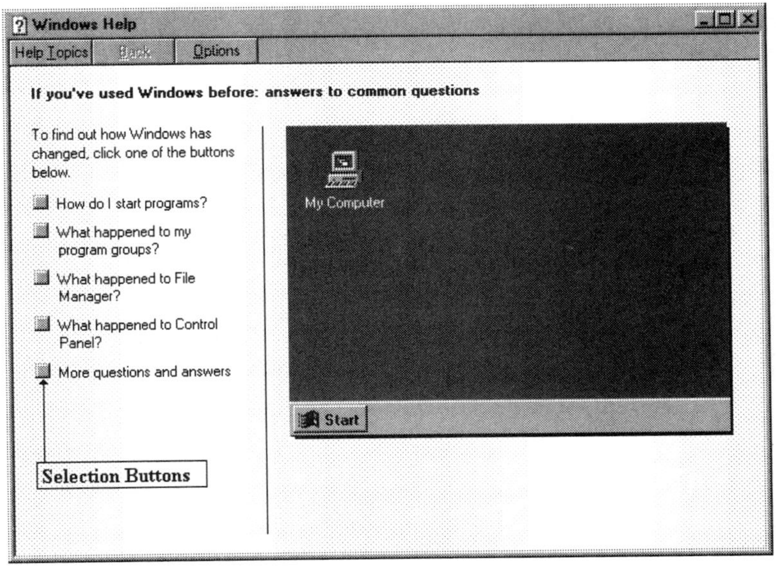

Figure 8–6: **Selection buttons let you pick from several topics.**

Getting Help for Dialog Boxes

➤*Right-clicking can help you understand dialog boxes.*

The help files discussed above are great for reading about a program, but you have to work to find information on specific dialog boxes. Many dialog boxes support a shortcut to the information you want. To access this information, right-click on the part of the dialog box in question. This will bring up a quick menu with one option, What's This? Click on this for an explanation of the particular item. You can see this in Figure 8–7. You can also get help on any part of a dialog box by clicking on the question mark button and then clicking on the item of interest.

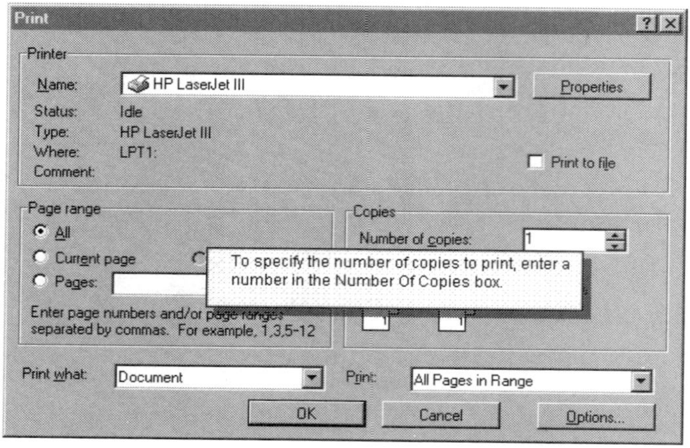

Figure 8–7: **By right-clicking, many dialog boxes can give you information about a specific item in the dialog box.**

Conclusion

The help system in Windows 95 and the programs that run under it make it easier to find answers to software questions while working at your computer.

Index

D

E

F

G

H